SUPPLEMENT
FOR THE YEARS 1930–1935
TO
A SHAKESPEARE
BIBLIOGRAPHY

SUPPLEMENT
FOR THE YEARS 1930-1935
TO
A SHAKESPEARE
BIBLIOGRAPHY

By

WALTHER EBISCH, PH.D.
LIBRARIAN OF THE ENGLISH SEMINAR
UNIVERSITY OF LEIPZIG

in collaboration with

LEVIN L. SCHÜCKING
PROFESSOR AT THE UNIVERSITY OF
LEIPZIG

Published by Benjamin Blom, Inc.
New York 1968

First published by Oxford University Press, 1936
Reissued 1964 by Benjamin Blom, Inc., NY 52
by permission of Oxford University Press
L. C. Catalog Card No.: 31-26966

Printed in U.S.A. by
NOBLE OFFSET PRINTERS, INC.
NEW YORK 3, N. Y.

PREFACE

SINCE the *Shakespeare Bibliography* was published in 1931, so many contributions to Shakespearian study have appeared in print that the necessity of a supplement to our former work makes itself felt. The subsequent pages follow the method and arrangement of the main work. They contain the new publications from 1930 to April 1936; furthermore, the opportunity has been taken to repair a few important omissions in the original work. The authors hope that the supplement will not meet with less approval and interest than the Bibliography itself; they would be grateful for any suggestions brought forward to fill in gaps or to improve the work done.

W. E.

L. L. S.

A. GENERAL

I. SHAKESPEARE BIBLIOGRAPHY

(*page* 1)[1]

Die Shakespeare-Literatur in Deutschland. Vollständiger Katalog sämtlicher in Deutschland erschienener Übersetzungen von 1762–1851. Supplement zu allen Übersetzungen und Erläuterungsschriften. Cassel, 1852. (44 S.)

WILLIAM THOMAS LOWNDES: Shakespeare. In his The bibliographer's manual of English literature. New edition by HENRY G. BOHN. London, 1864, vol. 4, pp. 2252–366.

F. D. MULLINS: Catalogue of the Shakespeare Memorial Library, Birmingham. Birmingham, 1872–6. (344 pp.)

APPLETON MORGAN: Digesta Shakespeareana. Being a topical index of printed matter (other than literary or aesthetic commentary or criticism) relating to William Shakespeare or the Shakespearean plays and poems. P. I, II. New York, 1887. (224 pp.)=Papers of the New York Shakespeare Society, nos. 4 and 7.

WALTHER EBISCH and LEVIN L. SCHÜCKING: A Shakespeare bibliography. O.U.P., 1931. (xviii, 294 pp.) Rev.: TLS. Feb. 19, 1931, p. 131; Bbl. 42, 1931, S. 97–9, W. Fischer; Börsenbl. f. d. Deutschen Buchhandel, 1931, No. 44, 21. Feb., S. 160–1, Rud. Hittmair; Observer, Sunday, May 3, 1931; Dt. Litztg. 1931, Sp. 1022–4, Friedr. Brie; Rev. anglo-amér. 8, 1931, pp. 440–1, E. Legouis; Rev. de litt. comp. 11, 1931, p. 542; Neophilologus, 16, 1931, S. 296–7, A. E. H. Swaen; Zentralbl. f. Bibliothekswesen, 48, 1931, S. 350, Joris Vorstius; RESt. 7, 1931, pp. 497–8, G. B. Harrison; Sh. Jb. 67, 1931, S. 90–1, W. Keller; Rev. crit. d'hist. et de litt. 65, 1931, p. 327, René Pruvost; JEGPh. 1932, pp. 150–2, Lawrence M. Price; MLR. 27, 1932, p. 114, H.B.C.; N.Spr. 40, 1932, S. 312–13, M. J. Wolff; E. St. 67, 1932, S. 121–3, H. M. Flasdieck; Litbl. 53, 1932, Sp. 238–41, Rob. Spindler; Libr., 4th ser., 11, 1931, pp. 510–11, A. W. Pollard.

II. ELIZABETHAN LITERATURE

(2) DICTIONARIES OF PLAYS AND DRAMATISTS

(*page* 3)

GERTRUDE MARIAN SIBLEY: The lost plays and masques, 1500–1642. Cornell Univ. Pr., 1933. (xiv, 205 pp.)=Cornell Studies in English, xix. Rev.: MLR. 29, 1934, pp. 193–5, W. W. Greg; RESt. 11, 1935, pp. 89–92, Mark Eccles; Bbl. 46, 1935, S. 119, W. Fischer.

W. P. BARRETT: Chart of plays, 1584–1623. New York, 1934. (40 pp.)

---

[1] The references throughout are to pages of the main bibliography.

(3) COLLECTIONS AND SPECIMENS OF THE DRAMA
(*page* 4)

Materials for the study of the old English drama. Ed. by HENRY DE VOCHT.

I. John Forde's Dramatic Works, reprinted from the original quartos. 2nd part. Ed. by H. DE VOCHT. 1928. (408 pp.)

II. CH. CRAWFORD: The Marlowe concordance. 4th part. 1929, pp. 521–680.

III. CH. CRAWFORD: The Marlowe concordance. 5th part. 1929, pp. 681–936.

IV. SIMON BAYLIE: The wizard. Ed. from the Durham and London MSS., with introd. and notes by HENRY DE VOCHT. Louvain, 1930. (cviii, 204 pp.)

V. Lust's Dominion. Ed. by LE GAY BRERETON. 1931. (xliv, 264 pp.)

VI. CH. CRAWFORD: The Marlowe concordance. 6th part. 1931, pp. 937–1192.

VII. CH. CRAWFORD: The Marlowe concordance. 7th part. 1932, pp. 1193–1454.

VIII. ROBERT GOMERSALL: The tragedie of Lodovick Sforza, Duke of Millan. Ed. from the quarto of 1628 by B. R. PEARN. 1933. (xxi, 135 pp.)

IX. BEN JONSON: Poetaster, or the Arraignment. Ed. by HENRY DE VOCHT. 1934. (viii, 142 pp.)

X. B. A. P. VAN DAM: The text of Shakespeare's Lear. 1935. (110 pp.)

The Malone Society Publications. Oxford, 1907 et seq.:

1930
The Two Noble Ladies, from MS. Egerton 1994.
The Rare Triumphs of Love and Fortune, 1589.

1931
King Johan, by JOHN BALE, from the Devonshire-Huntington MS.
Collections, Vol. II, Part iii, containing 'Processus Satanae', 'Somebody and Others', Players at Ipswich, Dramatic Records of the City of London and the Lord Chamberlain's Office.

1932
A Looking-glass for London and England, by THOMAS LODGE and ROBERT GREENE, 1594.
The Launching of the Mary, by WALTER MOUNTFORD (1632).

1933
Jack Juggler.
Alexander and Campaspe, by JOHN LYLY. (1584.)

E. H. C. OLIPHANT: Elizabethan dramatists other than Shakespeare. A selection of plays. New York, 1931. (xiv, 1511 pp.)

HAZELTON SPENCER: Elizabethan plays, written by Shakespeare's friends, colleagues, rivals, and successors, ed. with new texts based on the original folios, quartos, and octavos. Boston, 1933. (x, 1174 pp.) Rev.: MLN. 49, 1934, pp. 50–1, T. M. Parrott.

Authors represented: Christopher Marlowe, John Lyly, Robert Greene, Thomas Kyd, Ben Jonson, George Chapman, Thomas Dekker, John Marston, Thomas Heywood,

Francis Beaumont, John Fletcher, John Webster, Thomas Middleton, William Rowley, Philip Massinger, John Ford, James Shirley.

GEORGE RYLANDS: Elizabethan tragedy (excluding Shakespeare). London, 1933. (640 pp.)

CONTENTS: CHR. MARLOWE: Tamburlaine the Great. THOMAS HEYWOOD: A woman killed with kindness. CYRIL TOURNEUR: The revenger's tragedy. GEORGE CHAPMAN: Bussy d'Ambois. JOHN WEBSTER: The white devil. JOHN FORD: 'Tis pity she's a whore.

C. F. TUCKER BROOKE and NATHANIEL BURTON PARADISE: English drama, 1580–1642, selected and edited. Boston, 1933. (viii, 1044 pp.) Rev.: MLN. 49, 1934, pp. 193–4, Baldwin Maxwell.
Containing 29 plays.

Elizabethan and Stuart plays, ed. by C. R. BASKERVILL, V. B. HELTZEL, and A. H. NETHERCOT. New York, 1934. (x, 1660 pp.)

(4) GENERAL ACCOUNTS OF THE ELIZABETHAN DRAMA
(*page* 12)

WILLIAM HAZLITT: Lectures on the dramatic literature of the age of Elizabeth. London, 1820. Also in: Centenary Edition, ed. by P. P. HOWE. London, 1930 seq., vol. 6, pp. 169–364.

H. TAINE: Le théâtre anglais de la Renaissance. I, II. In: Revue germanique, vol. 25, 1863, pp. 209–53, 425–65.

HANS HECHT: Das elisabethanische Drama bis zum Auftreten Shakespeares. In: Shakespeares Werke. Übertr. nach Schlegel-Tieck von MAX J. WOLFF. Berlin, 1926, Bd. 22, S. 7–87.

E. A. GERRARD: Elizabethan drama and dramatists, 1583–1603. Oxford, 1928. (viii, 390 pp.)

FREDERICK S. BOAS: An introduction to Tudor drama. O.U.P., 1933. (viii, 176 pp.) Rev.: Revue anglo-amér. 11, 1933/4, pp. 151–2, A. Brulé; Engl. Studies, 18, 1936, pp. 27–9, W. A. Ovaa.

Le théâtre élizabéthain, publié sous la direction de GEORGETTE CAMILLE et PIERRE D'EXIDEUIL.=Cahiers du Sud, no. 154, 1933. (251 pp.)

W. P. BARRETT: Chart of plays, 1584–1623. C.U.P., 1934. (39 pp.)

KARL YOUNG: The drama of the medieval church. 2 vols. London, 1933. (xxii, 708 and 611 pp.) Rev.: MLN. 49, 1934, pp. 112–14, Grace Frank.

(5) VARIOUS TYPES OF DRAMA
(*a*) TRAGEDY
(*page* 14)

M. C. BRADBROOK: Themes and conventions of Elizabethan tragedy. C.U.P., 1935. (275 pp.) Rev.: Mod. Phil. 33, 1935, pp. 202–6, Gorley Putt.

(*c*) SCHOOL AND UNIVERSITY DRAMA
(*page* 15)

A. WIGFALL GREEN: The Inns of Court and early English drama. New Haven and O.U.P.,1931. (xiii,199 pp.) Rev.:RESt. 9,1933, pp. 218–21, W. J. Lawrence.

(d*) DOMESTIC DRAMA

(*page* 16)

P. NIEMEYER: Das bürgerliche Drama in England im Zeitalter Shakespeares. Diss. Göttingen, 1930. (105 S.)

(e) MASQUES

(*page* 16)

OSKAR FISCHEL: Inigo Jones und der Theaterstil der Renaissance. In: Bibliothek Warburg. Vorträge, 1930-1. Leipzig, 1932, S. 103-35 (m. 30 Taf.).

(f*) DRAMATIC BURLESQUE

(*page* 17)

GEORGE KITCHIN: A survey of burlesque and parody in English. London, 1931. (xxiv, 388 pp.)
Contains: Elizabethan dramatic burlesque (ch. ii, pp. 38-67).

(i) ENGLISH FOLK-PLAY

(*page* 18)

E. K. CHAMBERS: The English folk-play. O.U.P., 1933. (vi, 248 pp.) Rev.: MLR. 30, 1935, pp. 226-8, Enid Welsford.

(6) THE ELIZABETHAN DRAMATISTS AND THEIR MUTUAL RELATIONS

(a) COLLABORATION

(*page* 18)

FREDERICK E. PIERCE: The collaboration of Webster and Dekker. New York, 1909. (viii, 159 pp.)=Yale Studies in English, 37. Rev.: E. St. 45, 1912, S. 110-13, Ed. Eckhardt; Sh. Jb. 46, 1910, S. 295-7, Wolfg. Keller.

FREDERICK E. PIERCE: The collaboration of Dekker and Ford. In: Anglia, Bd. 36, 1912, S. 141-68 u. S. 289-312.

LOUIS WANN: The collaboration of Beaumont, Fletcher, and Massinger. In: Shakespeare Studies by members of the Department of English of the Univ. of Wisconsin. Madison, 1916, pp. 147-73.

S. R. GOLDING: Day and Wilkins as collaborators. In: N. & Q., vol. 150, 1926, pp. 237-9 and 259-62.

JOHANNES SCHLAF: Zur Frage der dichterischen Zusammenarbeit. In: Sh. Jb., Bd. 69, 1933, S. 102-11.

ALEXANDER TIEGS: Zur Zusammenarbeit englischer Berufsdramatiker unmittelbar vor, neben und nach Shakespeare. Diss. Breslau, 1933. (38 S.) Enlarged as: Beiträge zur Anglistik. Heft 2. (144 S.) Rev.: JEGPh. 34, 1935, pp. 118-19, T. W. Baldwin; Bbl. 46, 1935, S. 138-43, Elise Deckner; E. St. 70, 1936, S. 395-7, Max J. Wolff.

(b) PROBLEMS OF AUTHORSHIP

(*page* 18)

W. J. COURTHOPE: On the authenticity of some of the early plays assigned to Shakespeare, and their relationship to the development of his dramatic genius. In his History of English poetry, vol. 4, 1911, pp. 455–76 (Appendix).

J. M. ROBERTSON: The genuine in Shakespeare. A conspectus. London, 1930. (xi, 170 pp.) Rev.: Sh. Jb. 67, 1931, S. 88, W. Keller.
Here the author applies his tests of style and versification to all Shakespearian plays and he finds some alien matter in nearly all.

J. M. ROBERTSON: Marlowe. A conspectus. London, 1931. (186 pp.)
Cf. in particular: The assignable plays in the Folio (pp. 85–114), and Assignable collaborative work in the Folio (pp. 129–58).

E. H. C. OLIPHANT: The Shakespeare canon. In: Quart. Rev., vol. 259, 1932, pp. 32–48.

(c) THE WAR OF THE THEATRES

(*page* 19)

ROBERT BOIES SHARPE: The real war of the theaters. Shakespeare's fellows in rivalry with the Admiral's Men, 1594–1603. Repertories, devices, and types. O.U.P., 1935. (viii, 260 pp.)=The Mod. Lang. Ass. of America. Monograph Series, 5. Rev.: Bbl. 47, 1936, S. 118–27, L. L. Schücking.

(7) ELIZABETHAN LYRIC

(a) LYRICAL ANTHOLOGIES OF THE XVIth CENTURY

(*page* 19)

ARTHUR E. CASE: A bibliography of English poetical miscellanies, 1521–1750. O.U.P., 1935. (xi, 386 pp.) Rev.: TLS. Oct. 10, 1935, p. 626.

———

Tottel's Miscellany (1557): Songs and sonnetes by Henry Howard, Earl of Surrey, Sir Thomas Wyat the elder, Nicholas Grimald, and uncertain authors. First ed. of 15th June 1557, collated with the 2nd ed. of 31st July 1557, by EDWARD ARBER. London, 1870. (286 pp.)=English Reprints.

WALTER W. GREG: 'Tottel's Miscellany'. In: Libr. 1904, pp. 113–33.

Brittons Bowre of Delights, 1597. Text nebst Untersuchungen über Stil, Metrum und Verfasserschaft von H. KASSEBAUM. Diss. Göttingen, 1898. (39 S.)

Brittons Bowre of Delights (1591). Ed. by HYDER E. ROLLINS. Cambridge, Harv. Univ. Pr., 1933. (xxviii, 116 pp.)=Huntington Library Publications. Rev.: RESt. 11, 1935, pp. 96–8, H. J. Byrom; MLN. 50, 1935, pp. 115–17, Ernest A. Strathmann.
Collotype facsimile with introduction and notes.

The Phoenix Nest, 1593. Ed. by HYDER EDWARD ROLLINS. Harvard Univ. Pr., 1931. (xliii, 241 pp.) Rev.: TLS. June 18, 1931, p. 483; MLR. 27, 1932, pp. 213–14, Edith C. Batho; RESt. 8, 1932, pp. 330–3, H. J. Byrom.
Type-facsimile of the original.

England's Helicon, 1600, 1614. Ed. by HYDER EDWARD ROLLINS. Vol. I: Text. Vol. II: Introduction, notes, indexes. Harvard Univ. Pr., 1935.

A Poetical Rhapsody (1602–1621), containing diverse sonnets, odes, elegies, madrigals, and other poesies. Ed. by HYDER E. ROLLINS. Vols. I, II. Cambridge, Harv. Univ. Pr., 1931, 1932. (364 and 334 pp.) Rev.: RESt. 9, 1933, pp. 479–81, H. J. Byrom; MLR. 28, 1933, pp. 516–18, Geoffrey Tillotson; JEGPh. 32, 1933, pp. 619–20, H. S. V. J.

(b) MODERN ANTHOLOGIES

(*page* 20)

E. K. CHAMBERS: The Oxford book of 16th century verse. O.U.P., 1932. (906 pp.) Rev.: Rev. anglo-amér. 10, 1933, pp. 518–20, Floris Delattre.

(c) STUDIES IN THE ELIZABETHAN LYRIC

(*page* 20)

JOHN MURRAY GIBBON: Melody and the lyric from Chaucer to the Cavaliers. With 200 musical illustrations. London, 1930. (204 pp.)

(d) MADRIGALS

(*page* 21)

EDWARD FRANCIS RIMBAULT: Bibliotheca madrigaliana. London, 1847.

ORLANDO GIBBONS: Madrigals and motets. Originally published in parts, A.D. 1612, and now first printed in score. Edited by GEORGE SMART. London, Musical Antiquarian Soc., 1841.

JOHN DOWLAND: The first set of songs, scored from the first edition . . . 1597, and preceded by a life of the composer by W. CHAPPELL. London, Musical Antiquarian Soc., 1843.

F. A. COX: English madrigals in the time of Shakespeare. London, 1899. (292 pp.)

English madrigal verse, 1588–1632. Ed. by E. H. FELLOWES. O.U.P., [2]1929. (688 pp.)

HUGO HEURICH: John Wilbye in seinen Madrigalen. Studien zu einem Bilde seiner Persönlichkeit. Augsburg, 1932. (90 S. u. 88 Notenbeispiele.)= Veröff. d. musikwiss. Inst. d. dt. Univ. Prag. Heft 2. Rev.: Bbl. 45, 1934, S. 53–4, Hans Engel.

(f) PASTORAL POETRY

(*page* 22)

H. O. SOMMER: Die englische Hirtendichtung. Ein erster Versuch. Marburg, 1888. (131 S.)

WALTER W. GREG: Pastoral poetry and pastoral drama. A literary enquiry, with special reference to the Pre-Restoration stage in England. London, 1906. (xii, 464 pp.) Rev.: Sh. Jb. 43, 1907, S. 241–3, A. Brandl; MLR. 4, 1909, pp. 110–15, H. J. C. Grierson; Bbl. 18, 1907, S. 75–7, Ph. Aronstein. With good bibliography.

HECTOR GENOUY: L'élément pastoral dans la poésie narrative et le drame en Angleterre, de 1579-1640. Paris, 1929. (ix, 448 pp.)

(g) THE BALLAD
(*page* 22)

W. CHAPPELL: The ballad literature and popular music of the olden time. A history of the ancient songs, ballads, and of the dance tunes of England, etc., the airs harmonized by G. A. MACFARREN. 2 vols. London, 1859.

The Pepys Ballads, ed. by HYDER EDWARD ROLLINS. Vol. I, 1535-1625. London, 1929. (xix, 273 pp.) Rev.: MLR. 25, 1930, pp. 198-201, G. Thorn-Drury; TLS. June 12, 1930, p. 493; RESt. 6, 1930, pp. 369-71, F. Sidgwick.

(8) ELIZABETHAN NARRATIVE LITERATURE
(*page* 23)

Early English prose romances, ed. by WILLIAM J. THOMS. New edition. London, n.d. (958 pp.)

Shorter novels. Vol. I: Elizabethan and Jacobean. London, 1929. (xx, 356 pp.)=Everyman's Libr. 824.

Elizabethan prose. Selected and prefaced by MICHAEL ROBERTS. London, 1933. (376 pp.)

III. SHAKESPEARE'S LIFE
(1) DOCUMENTARY EVIDENCE
(*page* 23)

PIERCE BUTLER: Materials for the life of Shakespeare. Univ. of North Carolina Pr., 1930. (xi, 200 pp.) Rev.: JEGPh. 30, 1931, pp. 585-6, Tucker Brooke; Bbl. 44, 1933, S. 148-9, Ph. Aronstein.

E. K. CHAMBERS: William Shakespeare. A study of facts and problems. 2 vols. O.U.P., 1930. (xviii, 576 and xvi, 448 pp.) Rev.: RESt. 7, 1931, pp. 216-23, Ch. J. Sisson; MLR. 26, 1931, pp. 189-98, J. Dover Wilson; TLS. Oct. 23, 1930, p. 859; Libr. 1930, pp. 378-83, A. W. Pollard; N. Spr. 39, 1931, S. 463-7, M. J. Wolff; Litteris, 7, 1930, S. 137-43, L. L. Schücking; Sh. Jb. 67, 1931, S. 75-6, W. Keller; Mod. Phil. 29, 1932, pp. 370-3, C. R. Baskervill; Engl. Studies, 15, 1933, pp. 32-8, J. Kooistra.

LESLIE HOTSON: Shakespeare versus Shallow. London, 1931. (376 pp.) Rev.: TLS. Oct. 1, 1931, p. 749; Life and Letters, 7, 1931, pp. 356-62, Augustine Birrell; The Sh. Assoc. Bull. 6, 1931, pp. 183-4, Sam. A. Tannenbaum; Rev. anglo-amér. 9, 1932, pp. 224-32, F. C. Danchin; MLR. 27, 1932, pp. 218-21, W. W. Greg; Arch. 161, 1932, S. 115-16, A. Brandl; MLN. 47, 1932, pp. 399-402, Felix E. Schelling; The Sh. Assoc. Bull. 7, 1932, pp. 174-82, John E. Hannigan.

LESLIE HOTSON: Shakespeare and mine host of the Mermaid. In: Atlantic Monthly, 151, 1933, pp. 708–14.

Shows that the William Johnson, citizen and vintner of London, who witnessed Shakespeare's signature in the Blackfriars deed, was none other than mine host of the Mermaid.

CH. WILLIAMS: A short life of Shakespeare with the sources. Abridged from SIR EDMUND CHAMBERS's 'William Shakespeare. A study of facts and problems.' Oxford, 1933. (viii, 260 pp.) Rev.: Arch. Jg. 88, Bd. 164, S. 298–300, A. Brandl.

J. W. MACKAIL: The life of Shakespeare. In: A companion to Shakespeare studies. London, 1934, pp. 1–8.

(1*) SHAKESPEARE TRADITIONS
(*page* 23)

CHARLES FREDERICK GREEN: The legend of Shakespeare's crab-tree. London, 1857, 1862. (50 pp.)

CHARLES HOLTE BRACEBRIDGE: Shakespeare no deer-stealer, or a short account of Fulbroke Park, near Stratford-on-Avon. London, 1862. (iv, 32 pp.)

E. K. CHAMBERS: The Shakespeare-mythos. In his William Shakespeare. A study of facts and problems. O.U.P., 1930, vol. 2, pp. 238–302 (=Appendix C).

(2) SHAKESPEARE'S HANDWRITING
(*page* 24)

F. A. LEO: Shakespeares Ovid in der Bodleian Library zu Oxford. In: Sh. Jb. Jg. 16, 1881, S. 367–75.

SUPPLEMENT: SHAKESPEARE FORGERIES
(*page* 24)

E. K. CHAMBERS: Shakespearean fabrications. In his William Shakespeare. A study of facts and problems. O.U.P., 1930, vol. 2, pp. 377–93 (=Appendix F).

(a) THE IRELAND FORGERIES
(*page* 24)

SAMUEL IRELAND: An investigation of Mr. Malone's claim to the character of scholar, or critic, being an examination of his 'Inquiry into the authenticity of the Sh. manuscripts.' London, (1789?) (vi, 153 pp.)

DERK BODDE: Shakespeare and the Ireland forgeries. Harvard Univ. Pr., 1930. (68 pp.) Rev.: Sh. Jb. 67, 1931, S. 92–3, W. Keller.

(b) THE COLLIER FORGERIES
(*page* 25)

SAMUEL A. TANNENBAUM: Shaksperian scraps and other Elizabethan fragments. New York, 1933. (xvi, 217 pp.) Rev.: RESt. 10, 1934, pp. 464–8, A. K. McIlwraith; MLR. 30, 1935, pp. 87–90, Frederick S. Boas; Engl. Studies, 16, 1934, pp. 149–52, B. A. P. van Dam.

(c) THE SUPPOSED CUNNINGHAM FORGERIES
(*page* 26)

CHARLOTTE CARMICHAEL STOPES: Mr. W. J. Lawrence and Peter Cunningham. In: MLR., vol. 19, 1924, pp. 340–3.

T. W. BALDWIN: The Revels Books of 1604–5, and 1611–12. In: Libr., 4th ser., vol. 10, 1929/30, pp. 327–38.

A. E. STAMP: The disputed Revels Accounts, reproduced in collotype facsimile, with a paper read before the Shakespeare Assoc. O.U.P., for the Shakespeare Assoc., 1931. (16 and xxvi pp.) Rev.: TLS. March 5, 1931, p. 173; RESt. 8, 1932, pp. 104–5, Ch. J. Sisson; MLR. 27, 1932, pp. 87–8, W. J. Lawrence. 'We are on firm ground in trusting to the authenticity of these documents.'

(3) SHAKESPEARE'S NAME
(*page* 26)

C. FR. KOCH: Shakespere's name. In: Jb. f. roman. u. engl. Lit., Bd. 6, 1865, S. 322–6.

E. K. CHAMBERS: The name Shakespeare. In his William Shakespeare. A study of facts and problems. O.U.P., 1930, vol. 2, pp. 354–76 (=Appendix E).

(4) THE MOST IMPORTANT BIOGRAPHIES
(including general studies of Shakespeare's Life and Works)
(*page* 27)

NICHOLAS ROWE: Some account of the life and writings of Mr. William Shakespeare=Prefixed to his edition of the works of William Shakespeare. London, 1709.

JOHN DENNIS: Letters on the writings and genius of Shakespeare. London, 1712.

ELIZABETH MONTAGU: Essay on the writings and genius of Shakespeare, compared with the Greek and French dramatic poets. London, 1769. (iv, 288 pp.)

JOH. JOACHIM ESCHENBURG: Über W. Shakespeare. Zürich, 1787. (685 S.) ²1806.

EDMOND MALONE: The life of Shakespeare. In his 'Third Variorum Edition', 1821. Vol. 2, pp. 1–525.

AUGUSTINE SKOTTOWE: Life of Shakespeare. 2 vols. London, 1824.

HIPPOLYTE TAINE: Shakespeare. In his: Histoire de la littérature anglaise. Paris, 1863, ³1874 (T. 2, chap. 4, pp. 163–280).

THOMAS KENNY: The life and genius of Shakespeare. London, 1864. (viii, 414 pp.)

THOMAS DE QUINCEY: Shakespeare, a biography. London, 1864. (99 pp.)

VICTOR HUGO: William Shakespeare. Paris, 1864. (576 pp.) English translation by A. BAILLOT. London, 1864. German translation by A. DIEZMANN. Leipzig, 1864.

HAMILTON W. MABIE: William Shakespeare, poet, dramatist, and man. London, 1900. (xviii, 421 pp.) Rev.: Sh. Jb. 37, 1901, S. 241-2, G. B. Churchill.

W. TEIGNMOUTH SHORE: Shakespeare's self. London, 1920. (184 pp.)

ROMAN DYBOSKI: William Shakespeare. Krakau, 1927. (352 pp.) Rev.: Bbl. 41, 1930, S. 119-20, S. Helsztynski.

MARÍN L. ASTRANA: William Shakespeare. Madrid, 1930. (281 pp.)

E. K. CHAMBERS: William Shakespeare. A study of facts and problems. 2 vols. O.U.P., 1930. (xviii, 576 and xvi, 448 pp.) Rev.: RESt. 7, 1931, pp. 216-23, Ch. J. Sisson; MLR. 26, 1931, pp. 189-98, J. Dover Wilson; TLS. Oct. 23, 1930, p. 859; Libr. 1930, pp. 378-83, A. W. Pollard; N. Spr. 39, 1931, S. 463-7, M. J. Wolff; Litteris, 7, 1930, S. 137-43, L. L. Schücking; Sh. Jb. 67, 1931, S. 75-6, Wolfg. Keller; Mod. Phil. 29, 1932, pp. 370-3, C. R. Baskervill; E. St. 66, 1932, S. 418-23, Ed. Eckhardt; Bbl. 43, 1932, S. 97-103, Walther Fischer; Engl. Studies, 15, 1933, pp. 32-8, J. Kooistra.

CHRISTIAN GAEHDE: Shakespeare und seine Zeit. Eine Einführung in das Leben und die Werke des Dichters. Leipzig, 1931. (510 S.)

ALFONSO PAR: Vida de Shakespeare. Barcelona, 1931. (198 pp.)

JOHN DOVER WILSON: The essential Shakespeare. A biographical adventure. C.U.P., 1932. (viii, 148 pp.) Rev.: TLS. April 21, 1932, p. 287; MLR. 27, 1932, pp. 473-6, C. J. Sisson; RESt. 9, 1933, pp. 221-3, Mark Hunter.

JOHN DRINKWATER: Shakespeare. London, 1932. (118 pp.)

CHARLES WILLIAMS: A short life of Shakespeare with the sources. Abridged from SIR EDMUND CHAMBERS'S William Shakespeare. A study of facts and problems. Oxford, 1933. (viii, 260 pp.) Rev.: RESt. 10, 1934, pp. 469-70, G. B. Harrison.

DIEGO ANGELI: La vita di Guglielmo Shakespeare. Milano, 1934. (viii, 295 pp.) Rev.: Aevum, 9, 1935, pp. 224-5, Alberto Castelli.

(6) SHAKESPEARE'S FAMILY

(page 29)

L. L. SCHÜCKING: Shakespeares Vater. In: Neue Züricher Zeitung, 1927, S. 357.

ALFRED RANSFORD: John Hall, Shakespeare's son-in-law, and Hall of Idlicote. In: N. & Q., vol. 161, 1931, pp. 293-7 and 309-13.

FRANK MARCHAM: William Shakespeare and his daughter Susannah. London, 1931. (78 pp.)

(7) SHAKESPEARE'S SOCIAL ENVIRONMENT
(a) FRIENDS AND ACQUAINTANCES
(page 30)

E. A. B. BARNARD: New links with Shakespeare. C.U.P., 1930. (135 pp.) Rev.: Sh. Jb. 66, 1930, S. 214-15, W. Keller.

EDGAR I. FRIPP: Shakespeare studies, biographical and literary. O.U.P., 1930. (176 pp.) Rev.: Sh. Jb. 66, 1930, S. 216–17, W. Keller; MLR. 26, 1931, pp. 198–9, Ch. J. Sisson.

E. VINE HALL: Testamentary papers. I: Wills from Shakespeare's town and time. London, 1931. (40 pp.)

(b) COURT AND PATRONS
(*page* 31)

ARNOLD OSKAR MEYER: König Jakob I. Ein Charakterbild. In: Sh. Jb., Bd. 66, 1930, S. 6–24.

(c) LONDON AND SHAKESPEARE'S HOME
(*page* 31)

ROBERT E. HUNTER: Shakespeare and Stratford-on-Avon. A 'chronicle of the time', comprising the salient facts and traditions, biographical, topographical, and historical, connected with the poet and his birthplace. Stratford-on-Avon, 1864. (viii, 246 pp.)

BERTRAM C. A. WINDLE: Shakespeare's country. London, 1899. (xi, 219 pp.)

W. SALT BRASSINGTON: Shakespeare's homeland (illustrated). London, 1903. (xi, 356 pp.)

WILLIAM BAILEY KEMPLING: The Shakespeare memorials of London. London, 1923. (91 pp.) Rev.: TLS. April 26, 1923.

WILLIAM KENT: London for Shakespeare lovers. London, 1934. (180 pp.) Rev.: TLS. Aug. 23, 1934, p. 575.

(8) SHAKESPEARE ICONOGRAPHY
(a) PORTRAITS AND BUSTS
(*page* 31)

JAMES BOADEN: An inquiry into the authenticity of various pictures and prints which, from the decease of the poet to our own times, have been offered to the public as portraits of Shakespeare. London, 1824. (viii, 206 pp.)

JAMES H. FRISWELL: Life portraits of William Shakespeare. A history of the various representations of the poet, with an examination into their authenticity. Illustrated by photographs, etc. London, 1864. (xii, 128 pp.)

J. PARKER NORRIS: The portraits of Shakespeare. Philadelphia, 1885. (xxviii, 266 pp.)

M. H. SPIELMANN: 'This figure, that thou here seest put.' In: A book of homage to Shakespeare, ed. by ISRAEL GOLLANCZ. London, 1916, pp. 3–12.

SAMUEL A. TANNENBAUM: The Ashbourne portrait. In: The Shakespeare Assoc. Bull., vol. 5, 1930, pp. 123–5.

IV. SHAKESPEARE'S PERSONALITY

(1) GENERAL ACCOUNT OF SHAKESPEARE'S CHARACTER

(page 32)

WALTER BAGEHOT: Shakespeare—the man. 1853. Repr. in his Literary studies. Everyman's Libr., vol. 1, pp. 112–53.

H. C. BEECHING: The benefit of the doubt. In: A book of homage to Shakespeare, ed. by ISRAEL GOLLANCZ. London, 1916, pp. 120–5.

G. WILSON KNIGHT: Myth and miracle. An essay on the mystic symbolism of Shakespeare. London, 1929. (32 pp.)

CUMBERLAND CLARK: The eternal Shakespeare. London, 1930. (256 pp.)

(2) SHAKESPEARE'S CONCEPTION OF LIFE AND THE WORLD

(a) SHAKESPEARE'S PHILOSOPHICAL IDEAS IN GENERAL

(page 33)

J. CHURTON COLLINS: Sophocles and Shakespeare as theological and ethical teachers. In his Studies in Shakespeare. London, 1904, pp. 127–79.

HEINRICH MUTSCHMANN: Shakespeares Weltanschauung. In: Shakespeares Werke. Übertr. nach Schlegel-Tieck von MAX J. WOLFF. Berlin, 1926, Bd. 22, S. 153–202.

WILHELM BORNSCHEUER: Doppeldeutigkeit und Widersinn in Natur und Leben bei Shakespeare. Disc. Marburg, 1929. (53 S.)

HARDIN CRAIG: Shakespeare and formal logic. In: Studies in Philology. A miscellany in honor of Frederick Klaeber. Minneapolis, 1929, pp. 330–97.

RENÉ BERTHELOT: La sagesse de Shakespeare et de Goethe. Paris, 1930. (239 pp.) Rev.: TLS. March 5, 1931, p. 177.

MAX DEUTSCHBEIN: Individuum und Kosmos in Shakespeares Werken. In: Sh. Jb., Bd. 69, 1933, S. 6–26.

MAX J. WOLFF: Shakespeares Stellung an der Grenze zweier Zeiten. In: GRM. Jg. 21, 1933, S. 425–38.

ALLAN H. GILBERT: Logic in the Elizabethan drama. In: Stud. in Phil., vol. 32, 1935, pp. 527–45.

(b) SHAKESPEARE'S PSYCHOLOGY AND ETHICS

(page 34)

V. KNAUER: Shakespeare der Philosoph der sittlichen Weltordnung. Innsbruck, 1879. (371 S.)

LILY B. CAMPBELL: Shakespeare's tragic heroes, slaves of passion. C.U.P., 1930. (xii, 248 pp.) Rev.: TLS. Jan. 1, 1931, p. 9; Engl. Studies, 13, 1931, pp. 111–18, J. Kooistra; E. St. 66, 1931, S. 268–73, Ed. Eckhardt; Sh. Jb. 67, 1931, S. 83–4, Wolfg. Keller; MLR. 27, 1932, pp. 82–4, H. B. Charlton; Bbl. 43, 1932, S. 115–17, H. Jantzen.

WILLIAM WITHERLE LAWRENCE: Shakespeare's problem comedies. New York, 1931. (xi, 259 pp.) Rev.: TLS. July 16, 1931, pp. 554–5; Sh. Jb. 67, 1931, S. 82–3, Wolfg. Keller.
Deals with Shakespeare's moral principles in All's, Meas., Troil., and Cymb.

HEINZ NICOLAI: 'Ecstasy' und 'passion'. Ein Beitrag zur Deutung des Hamletcharakters. In: GRM. Jg. 23, 1935, S. 37–67.

ANDRÉ ADNÈS: Shakespeare et la pathologie mentale. Thèse, Paris, 1935. (247 pp.)

(3) SHAKESPEARE'S ATTITUDE TOWARDS RELIGION AND THE CHURCH
(page 35)

JAMES BROWN: Bible truths, with Shakespearian parallels. London, 1862, ²1864. (xxiii, 207 pp.)

CHARLES ALFRED SWINBURNE: Sacred and Shakespearian affinities, being analogies between the writings of the psalmists and of Shakespeare. London, 1890.

WILLIAM BARRY: The Catholic strain in Shakespeare. In: A book of homage to Shakespeare, ed. by ISRAEL GOLLANCZ. London, 1916, pp. 31–4.

FELIX LIEBERMANN: Shakespeares Anschauung von Staat, Gesellschaft und Kirche in Heinrich VIII. In: Beitr. zur Lit. u. Theatergeschichte, Ludwig Geiger z. 70. Geb. Berlin, 1918, S. 13 ff.

CLEMENT C. J. WEBB: Shakespeare and religion. In: Hibbert Journal, vol. 26, 1927/8, pp. 341–54.

W. C. PROCTOR: Shakespeare and Scripture. London, 1929. (48 pp.)

MARK HUNTER: Spiritual values in Shakespeare. In: Speculum religionis. Being essays and studies in religion and literature from Plato to von Hügel, presented to Claude G. Montefiore. O.U.P., 1929.

FEDERICO OLIVERO: Shakespeare in rapporto alla religione ed alla morale. In: Rivista di filosofia neo-scolastica, vol. 23, 1933, pp. 548–61.

RICHMOND NOBLE: Shakespeare's biblical knowledge and use of the Book of Common Prayer, as exemplified in the plays of the First Folio. London, 1935. (xii, 304 pp.)

(4) SHAKESPEARE'S ATTITUDE TOWARDS THE SUPERNATURAL
(page 36)

FRANCIS DOUCE: Illustrations of Shakespeare and of ancient manners, with dissertations on the clowns and fools of Shakespeare. 2 vols. London, 1807, ²1839.

JOSEPH RITSON: Fairy tales, legends and romances illustrating Shakespeare and other early English writers. To which are prefixed two preliminary dissertations (1) on pigmies, (2) on fairies. London, 1831, 1875. (426 pp.)

ALFRED ROFFE: An essay upon the ghost-belief of Shakespeare. London, 1851. (32 pp.)

WILLIAM BELL: Shakespeare's Puck and his folklore, illustrated from the superstitions of all nations. 3 vols. London, 1852–64.

BENNO TSCHISCHWITZ: Nachklänge germanischer Mythe in den Werken Shakespeares. Halle, 1865.

WILLIAM CAREW HAZLITT: Fairy tales, legends, and romances, illustrating Shakespeare and other early English writers. London, 1875.

IRENE ZOCCO: Il folk-lore di Shakespeare. In her *Spigolando*. Catania, 1900.

HERMANN SCHELENZ: Shakespeare und sein Wissen auf den Gebieten der Arznei- und Volkskunde. Bd. 1. Leipzig und Hamburg, 1914. (vii, 328 S.) Rev.: Sh. Jb. 52, 1916, S. 217–25, M. Förster.

EUSTACHE F. BOSANQUET: English printed almanacks and prognostications. A bibliographical history to the year 1600. London, Bibliographical Soc., 1917.

MINOR WHITE LATHAM: The Elizabethan fairies. The fairies of folklore and the fairies of Shakespeare. New York, Columbia Univ. Pr., 1930. (313 pp.) Rev.: RESt. 8, 1932, pp. 102–3, M. A. Murray; TLS. April 23, 1931, p. 322.

HEINRICH HÖHNA: Der Physiologus in der elisabethanischen Literatur. Diss. Erlangen, 1930. (88 S.)

CUMBERLAND CLARK: Shakespeare and the supernatural. London, 1931. (346 pp.) Rev.: TLS. Dec. 10, 1931, p. 999.

CARROLL CAMDEN: Elizabethan almanacs and prognostications. In: Libr., vol. 12, 1931, pp. 83–108 and 194–207.

FREDERICK T. WOOD: The supernatural in the Shakespearean drama. In: Rev. anglo-amér., vol. 9, 1932, pp. 200–17.

CARROLL CAMDEN, JR.: Astrology in Shakespeare's day. In: Isis, vol. 19, 1933, pp. 26–73.

(5) SHAKESPEARE'S ATTITUDE TOWARDS THE STATE

(page 38)

R. SIMPSON: The political use of the stage in Shakespeare's time. In: Publ. New Sh. Soc., 1874, pp. 371–95.

EDWARD SALMON: Shakespeare and democracy. London, 1916. (60 pp.)

FELIX LIEBERMANN: Shakespeares Anschauung von Staat, Gesellschaft und Kirche in Heinrich VIII. In: Beitr. z. Lit. u. Theatergeschichte, Ludwig Geiger z. 70. Geb. Berlin, 1918, S. 13 ff.

WILHELM HOLZHAUSEN: Übersee in den Darstellungsformen des elisabethanischen Dramas. Breslau, 1928=Beitr. z. Erforschung d. Sprache u. Kultur Englands u. Nordamerikas. Bd. 4, S. 155–227.

AGNES HENNEKE: Shakespeares englische Könige im Lichte staatsrechtlicher Strömungen seiner Zeit. In: Sh. Jb., Jg. 66, 1930, S. 79–144. (=Diss. Münster, 1930.)

WOLFGANG CLEMEN: Shakespeare und das Königtum. In: Sh. Jb., Bd. 68, 1932, S. 56–79.

PAUL ADAMS: Shakespeare als politischer Dichter. In: Dt. Volkstum. Jg. 15, 1933, S. 945–53.

GERHARD PALETTA: Fürstengeschick und innerstaatlicher Machtkampf im englischen Renaissance-Drama. Breslau, 1934. (128 S.) Rev.: Sh. Jb. 71, 1935, S. 120-1, Wolfg. Keller.
Cf. in particular chapter E: 'Die Idee des Tragischen bei Shakespeare und der Verstoss des einzelnen gegen die Gemeinschaft', S. 58–85.

RICHARD V. LINDABURY: A study of patriotism in the Elizabethan drama. Princeton Univ. Pr., 1931. (viii, 218 pp.)=Princeton Studies in English, no. 5. Rev.: MLN. 47, 1932, pp. 404–6, Ray Heffner.

FRANZ GROSSE: Das englische Renaissancedrama im Spiegel zeitgenössischer Staatstheorien. Breslau, 1935. (ix, 95 S.)=Sprache u. Kultur d. germ. u. roman. Völker, A, 18.

ALFRED HART: Shakespeare and the homilies. Melbourne and London, 1934. (262 pp.)

JOHN W. DRAPER: Political themes in Shakespeare's later plays. In: JEGPh., vol. 35, 1936, pp. 61–93.

(6) SHAKESPEARE'S ATTITUDE TOWARDS THE SOCIAL CLASSES

(*page* 39)

FREDERICK T. WOOD: Shakespeare and the plebs. In: Essays and Studies by members of the Engl. Assoc., vol. 18, 1933, pp. 53–73.

SAMUEL A. TANNENBAUM: Shakspere's caste prejudices. A reply to Ernest Crosby. In his Shaksperian scraps and other Elizabethan fragments. New York, 1933, pp. 153–76.

JOHN W. DRAPER: Court vs. country in Shakespeare's plays. In: JEGPh., vol. 33, 1934, pp. 222–32.

M. ST. CLARE BYRNE: The social background. In: A companion to Shakespeare studies. C.U.P., 1934, pp. 187–218.

JOHN W. DRAPER: La vie sociale élizabéthaine dans les pièces de Shakespeare. In: Rev. de l'enseignement des langues vivantes, vol. 51, 1934, pp. 392–402.

(7) SHAKESPEARE'S ATTITUDE TOWARDS THE LAW

(*page* 39)

WILLIAM L. RUSHTON: Shakespeare a lawyer. London, 1858. (50 pp.)

WILLIAM L. RUSHTON: Shakespeare's testamentary language. London, 1869. (viii, 56 pp.)

GEORGE W. KEETON: Shakespeare and his legal problems. London, 1930. (x, 239 pp.) Rev.: TLS. May 29, 1930, p. 452.

(8) SHAKESPEARE'S ATTITUDE TOWARDS NATURE AND SCIENCE

(a) NATURE AND SCIENCE IN GENERAL

(*page* 40)

CUMBERLAND CLARK: Shakespeare and science. A study of Shakespeare's interest in, and literary and dramatic use of, natural phenomena; with an account of the astronomy, astrology, and alchemy of his day. Birmingham, 1929. (262 pp.) Rev.: TLS. Feb. 13, 1930, p. 121; Dt. Litztg. 51, 1930, Sp. 2184-6, F. Krog; Bbl. 43, 1932, S. 113-15, H. Jantzen.

HEINRICH HÖHNA: Der Physiologus in der elisabethanischen Literatur. Diss. Erlangen, 1930. (89 S.)

(b) ZOOLOGY

(*page* 40)

A. GEIKIE: The birds of Shakespeare. Glasgow, 1916. (x, 122 pp.)

(c) BOTANY

(*page* 41)

LEO H. GRINDON: The Shakspere flora. A guide to all the principal passages in which mention is made of trees, plants, flowers and vegetable productions. With comments and botanical particulars. Manchester, 1883. (xii, 318 pp.)

ELEANOUR SINCLAIR ROHDE: Shakespeare's wild flowers. Fairy lore, gardens, herbs, gatherers of simples and bee lore. London, 1935.

(d) MEDICINE

(*page* 41)

JOHN MOYES: Medicine and kindred arts in the plays of Shakespeare. Glasgow, 1896. (xiv, 124 pp.)

A. E. HOCHE: Shakespeare und die Psychiatrie. In his *Aus der Werkstatt*. München, 1935, S. 25-37.

(9) SHAKESPEARE'S ATTITUDE TOWARDS ART

(*page* 41)

CARL VAN DOREN: Shakspere on his art. In: Shakespearian studies, ed. by B. MATTHEWS and A. H. THORNDIKE. New York, 1916, pp. 405-27.

EDWARD J. DENT: Shakespeare and music. In: A companion to Shakespeare studies. C.U.P., 1934, pp. 137-61.

KARL WOERMANN: Shakespeare und die bildenden Künste. Leipzig, 1930 (viii, 138 S.)=Abhdl. Sächs. Akad. Wiss., Bd. 41, 1930, no. 3. Rev.: Bbl. 44, 1933, S. 102-4, B. Fehr.

MARGARET FARRAND THORP: Shakespeare and the fine arts. In: PMLA., vol 46, 1931, pp. 672-93.

(11) SHAKESPEARE'S GEOGRAPHICAL KNOWLEDGE. HIS ALLEGED TRAVELS

(page 42)

THEODOR ELZE: Italienische Skizzen zu Shakespeare. In: Sh. Jb., Jg. 13, 1878, S. 137–57; 14, 1879, S. 156–79; 15, 1880, S. 230–65.

GREGOR SARRAZIN: Neue italienische Skizzen zu Shakespeare. In: Sh. Jb., Jg. 31, 1895, S. 165–76; 36, 1900, S. 95–108; 39, 1903, S. 62–8; 42, 1906, S. 179–86.

JAN STEFANSSON: Shakespeare at Elsinore. In: Contemp. Rev., vol. 69, 1896, no. 361.

WOLFGANG KELLER: Zu Shakespeares italienischer Reise. In: Sh. Jb., Jg. 35, 1899, S. 260–4.

GREGOR SARRAZIN: Shakespeare in Mailand? In: Sh. Jb., Jg. 46, 1910, S. 114–17.

VIOLET M. JEFFERY: Shakespeare's Venice. In: MLR., vol. 27, 1932, pp. 24–35.

E. G. R. TAYLOR: Late Tudor and early Stuart geography, 1583–1650. London, 1934. (ix, 322 pp.)

(12) SHAKESPEARE AND SPORT

(page 43)

HENRY NICHOLSON ELLACOMBE: Shakespeare as an angler. London, 1883. (78 pp.)

WILLIAM L. RUSHTON: Shakespeare an archer. Liverpool, 1897. (118 pp.)

CARLETON BROWN: Shakespeare and the horse. In: Libr., 3rd ser., vol. 3, 1912, pp. 152–80.

(13) SHAKESPEARE AND HERALDRY

(page 43)

GUY CADOGAN ROTHERY: The heraldry of Shakespeare. A commentary with annotations. London, 1930. (115 pp.) Rev.: TLS. Oct. 30, 1930, p. 889.

(14) SHAKESPEARE AND WOMEN (Love, Marriage, Family)

(page 43)

[Anon.]: Shakespeare and love. In: TLS. Oct. 13, 1921, pp. 649–50.

MORTON LUCE: Shakespeare, a vindication. In: Fortn. Rev., 1928, pp. 479–92.

GEORGE WILLIAM GERWIG: Shakespeare's ideals of womanhood. East Aurora, N.Y., 1929. (229 pp.)

ARTHUR QUILLER-COUCH: Paternity in Shakespeare. O.U.P., 1932. (20 pp.)= Brit. Acad. Annual Shakespearian Lecture.

LU EMILY PEARSON: Elizabethan love conventions. California Univ. Pr., 1933. (xi, 365 pp.) Rev.: MLR. 29, 1934, pp. 191–2, H. S. Bennett.

(15) SHAKESPEARE'S ATTITUDE TOWARDS VARIOUS PROBLEMS

HENRY W. FARNAM: Shakespeare's economics. New Haven, Yale Univ. Pr., 1931. (xv, 188 pp.) Rev.: TLS. Oct. 29, 1931, p. 836.

V. TEXT: TRANSMISSION AND EMENDATION

(1) PRINTING OF WORKS IN SHAKESPEARIAN TIMES

(a) PRINTING IN GENERAL AND THE TRANSMISSION OF SHAKESPEARE'S TEXT

(page 44)

WILLIAM BLADES: Common typographical errors, with special reference to the text of Shakespeare. In: Athenaeum, 1872, vol. 1, p. 114.

W. F. WYNDHAM BROWN: The origin and growth of copyright. In: Law Magazine and Review, 1909, pp. 54–65.

WILLIAM POEL: Shakespeare's prompt copies. In: TLS. Feb. 3, 1921, pp. 75–6.

WALTER W. GREG: An Elizabethan printer and his copy. In: Trans. Bibliogr. Soc., 1923, pp. 102–18.

RONALD B. MCKERROW: An introduction to bibliography for literary students. O.U.P., 1927. (xv, 359 pp.)

FRANK ARTHUR MUMBY: The book trade under Queen Elizabeth. In his: Publishing and bookselling. London, 1930, pp. 67–89.

R. B. MCKERROW: The Elizabethan printer and dramatic manuscripts. In: Libr., vol. 12, 1931, pp. 253–75.

TUCKER BROOKE: Elizabethan proof corrections in a copy of 'The First Part of the Contention', 1600. In: The Huntington Libr. Bull. 1931, no. 2, pp. 87–9, with 8 pp. in collotype.

JOSEPH Q. ADAMS: Elizabethan playhouse manuscripts and their significance for the text of Shakespeare. In: Johns Hopkins Alumni Mag., vol. 21, 1932, pp. 21–52.

CYRIL BATHURST JUDGE: Elizabethan book-pirates. Cambridge, Harv. Univ. Pr., 1934. (xiv, 198 pp.)=Harv. Studies in English. 8.
Deals in particular with the piracy of psalm-books, A B C's, and grammars.

A. W. POLLARD: Shakespeare's text. In: A companion to Shakespeare studies. C.U.P., 1934, pp. 263–86.

PERCY SIMPSON: Proof-reading in the 16th, 17th, and 18th centuries. O.U.P., 1935. (264 pp.) Rev.: RESt. 11, 1935, pp. 475–9, W. W. Greg; JEGPh. 34, 1935, pp. 595–7, T. W. Baldwin.

R. B. MCKERROW: A suggestion regarding Shakespeare's manuscripts. In: RESt., vol. 11, 1935, pp. 459–65.
The plays in which the names are irregular were printed from the author's MS., the uniform names point to the fair copy of a professional scribe.

ALFRED E. HARBAGE: Elizabethan and 17th century play manuscripts. In: PMLA., vol. 50, 1935, pp. 687–99.
A list of more than 200 play MSS. dating from 1558 to 1700.

CROMPTON RHODES: Some aspects of Sheridan bibliography. In: Libr., 4th ser., vol. 9, 1928, pp. 233–61.

(b) PRINTERS, PUBLISHERS, AND BOOKSELLERS
(*page* 45)

WILLIAM JAGGARD: Shakespeare's publishers. Notes on the Tudor-Stuart period of the Jaggard Press. Liverpool, 1907. (12 pp.)

HILARY JENKINSON: English current writing and early printing. In: Trans. Bibliogr. Soc., vol. 13, 1916, pp. 273–95.

RONALD B. MCKERROW: Edward Alde as a typical trade printer. In: Libr., 1929/30, pp. 121–62.

Records of the Court of the Stationers' Company, 1576–1602, from Register B. Ed. by W. W. GREG and ELEANORE BOSWELL. London, 1930. (lxxxii, 144 pp.) Rev.: MLR. 26, 1931, pp. 455–6, W. L. Renwick; RESt. 8, 1932, pp. 106–8, E. E. Willoughby.
Greg's introduction is the best available discussion of the organization of the Stationers' Company during the Elizabethan period.

FRANK ARTHUR MUMBY: Shakespeare's publishers. In his Publishing and bookselling. London, 1930, pp. 90–105.

A. E. M. KIRWOOD: Richard Field, printer, 1589–1624. In: Libr., vol. 12, 1931, pp. 1–39.

R. B. MCKERROW: The Elizabethan printer and dramatic manuscripts. In: Libr., vol. 12, 1931, pp. 253–75.

HARRY R. HOPPE: John Wolfe, printer and publisher, 1579–1601. In: Libr., vol. 14, 1933, pp. 241–88.

HENRIETTA C. BARTLETT: Extant autograph material by Shakespeare's fellow dramatists. In: Libr., vol. 10, 1929, pp. 308–12.

EDWIN ELIOTT WILLOUGHBY: A printer of Shakespeare: the books and times of William Jaggard. London, 1934. (xvi, 304 pp.) Rev.: TLS. Oct. 25, 1934, p. 731.

(c) ELIZABETHAN HANDWRITING
(*page* 47)

SAMUEL A. TANNENBAUM: The handwriting of the Renaissance. Being the development and characteristics of the script of Shakspere's time. New York and London, 1930. (xii, 210 pp.) Rev.: JEGPh. 31, 1932, pp. 148–50, Tucker Brooke.

(d) ELIZABETHAN SHORTHAND
(*page* 48)

H. T. PRICE: Another shorthand sermon. In: Essays and studies in English and comparative literature, by members of the English Department of the Univ. of Michigan, 1933. _____

CURT DEWISCHEIT: Shakespeare und die Anfänge der englischen Stenographie. Ein Beitrag zur Genesis der Shakespeare-Dramen. Berlin, 1897. (42 S.)

WERNER KRANER: Zur englischen Kurzschrift im Zeitalter Shakespeares. Das Jane Seager-Manuskript. (The Divine Prophecies of the Ten Sibyls.) In: Sh. Jb., Bd. 67, 1931, S. 26–61.

W. MATTHEWS: Shorthand and the bad Shakespeare quartos. In: MLR., vol. 27, 1932, pp. 243–62; postscript: 28, 1933, pp. 81–3.

RUDOLF WEINMEISTER: Die Bedeutung der Brightschen Kurzschrift für die Überlieferung der Shakespeare-Dramen. In: Mitteilungen des österr. Berufsstenographen-Verbandes. 1932, no. 77.

MAX FÖRSTER: Zur Shakespeare-Stenographie. In: Sh. Jb., Bd. 68, 1932, S. 87–102.

JOSEPH QUINCY ADAMS: The quarto of King Lear and shorthand. In: Mod. Phil., vol. 31, 1933, pp. 135–63.

MADELEINE DORAN: The quarto of King Lear and Bright's shorthand. In: Mod. Phil., vol. 33, 1935, pp. 139–57.

W. MATTHEWS: Peter Bales, Timothy Bright and William Shakespeare. In: JEGPh., vol. 34, 1935, pp. 483–510.
The author comes to the conclusion that Bales's Brachygraphy deserves the same consideration as Bright's method.

(e) CENSORSHIP IN ELIZABETHAN TIMES
(page 48)

ERNEST KUHL: The Stationers' Company and censorship (1599–1601). In: Libr., N.S., vol. 9, 1929, pp. 388–94.

ALFRED HART: Was the second part of King Henry the Fourth censored? In his Shakespeare and the homilies. O.U.P., 1934, pp. 154–218.

WILLIAM M. CLYDE: Struggle for the freedom of the press from Caxton to Cromwell. London and New York, 1934. (xvi, 360 pp.) Rev.: MLR. 30, 1935, pp. 513–14, W. W. Greg.

(f) SOCIAL POSITION OF WRITERS
(page 49)

WILLIAM C. HAZLITT: Prefaces, dedications, and epistles selected from early books, 1540–1701. London, privately printed, 1874.

CLARA GEBERT: An anthology of Elizabethan dedications and prefaces. Philadelphia, 1933. (ix, 302 pp.)

———

H. B. WHEATLEY: The dedication of books to patron and friend. London, 1887.

B. B. GAMZUE: Elizabeth and literary patronage. In: PMLA., vol. 49, 1934, pp. 1041–9.
Destroys the tradition of Elizabeth being a patron of the arts.

(2) OLDEST PRINTED TEXTS. FOLIOS AND QUARTOS
(a) BIBLIOGRAPHY OF OLDEST TEXTS IN GENERAL
(page 49)

JUSTIN WINSOR: Bibliography of the original quartos and folios of Shakespeare, with particular reference to copies in America. Boston, 1876. (110 pp. and 68 facs.)

The John Rylands Library, Manchester. Catalogue of an exhibition of the works of Shakespeare, his sources, and the writings of his principal contemporaries. Tercentenary of the death of Shakespeare, 1616. Manchester Univ. Pr., 1916. (xvi, 169 pp.)

(b) THE FOUR FOLIOS

a. THE FIRST FOLIO

(aa) Reprints
(page 50)

Shakespeare, as put forth in 1623. A reprint of Mr. William Shakespeare's comedies, histories and tragedies. Published according to the true original copies. London, LIONEL BOOTH, 1864. (xvi, 993 pp.)

(bb) Studies
(page 51)

JOSEPH QUINCY ADAMS: Timon of Athens and the irregularities of the First Folio. In: JEGPh., vol. 7, 1907–8, pp. 53–63.

EDWIN ELIOTT WILLOUGHBY: The printing of the First Folio of Shakespeare. O.U.P., for the Bibliogr. Soc., 1932. (xvi, 70 pp.)=Trans. Bibliogr. Soc., Suppl. no. 8. Rev.: TLS. July 13, 1933, p. 476.

EDWARD D. JOHNSON: The First Folio of Shakespeare. London, 1932. (91 pp.)

(c) THE QUARTOS
(page 52)

A. W. POLLARD and J. DOVER WILSON: 'The stolne and surreptitious copies'. In: TLS. 1919, pp. 13, 20, 134, 420, 434.

E. K. CHAMBERS: Table of quartos. In his William Shakespeare. A study of facts and problems. O.U.P., 1930, vol. 2, pp. 394–6 (=Appendix G).

W. J. LAWRENCE: The secret of 'the bad quartos'. In: New Criterion, vol. 10, 1931, pp. 447–61.

HENRIETTA C. BARTLETT: First editions of Shakespeare's quartos. In: Libr., N.S., vol. 16, 1935, pp. 166–72.
A revised list of present owners of all known copies.

Supplement: THE QUESTION OF THE QUARTO EDITIONS OF 1619 ('PAVIER'S COLLECTION')
(page 53)

ALBRECHT WAGNER: Eine Sammlung von Shakespeares Quartos in Deutschland. In: Anglia, Bd. 25, 1902, S. 518–32.

A. W. POLLARD: False dates in Shakespeare quartos. In: Libr., 3rd ser., vol. 2, 1911, pp. 101–7.

DUDLEY HUTCHERSON: The forged quartos. In: TLS. Jan. 3, 1935, p. 9.

(3) LATER EDITIONS WITH CRITICAL TEXT REVISION

(a) GENERAL LITERATURE

(*page* 53)

W. R. ARROWSMITH: Shakespeare's editors and commentators. London, 1865. (52 pp.)

HARRISON ROSS STEEVES: American editors of Shakspere. In: Shaksperian studies. Ed. by B. MATTHEWS and A. H. THORNDIKE. New York, 1916, pp. 347–68.

(b) EDITIONS

(*page* 53)

1709–10. ROWE.

Cf. also: ALFRED JACKSON: Rowe's edition of Shakespeare. In: Libr., N.S., vol. 10, 1930, pp. 455–73. R. B. MCKERROW: Rowe's Shakespeare, 1709. In: TLS. March 8, 1934, p. 168.

1733. THEOBALD.

Cf. also: EDWARD B. KOSTER: Lewis Theobald. In: Engl. Studies, vol. 4, 1922, pp. 20–31 and 49–60.

1747. WARBURTON.

A. W. EVANS: Warburton and the Warburtonians. A study in some 18th century controversies. O.U.P., 1932. (viii, 315 pp.)
Cf. in particular chap. ix: Edition of Shakespeare; Theobald; Hanmer, Thomas Edwards; Dr. Johnson (pp. 143–64).

1790. MALONE.

JOSEPH RITSON: Cursory criticisms on the edition of Shakespeare, published by Edmond Malone. London, 1792. (x, 104 pp.)

1847. The plays of William Shakespeare, from the text of George Steevens and Edmond Malone, with notes, a history of the stage and a life of Shakespeare by ALEXANDER CHALMERS. 8 vols. London, 1847.

1857–65. The works of William Shakespeare. The plays edited from the Folio of 1623, with various readings from all the editions and all the commentators, notes, introductory remarks, a historical sketch of the text, an account of the rise and progress of the English drama, a memoir of the poet, and an essay upon his genius, by RICHARD GRANT WHITE. 12 vols. Boston, 1857–65.

1864. The plays of Shakespeare, carefully edited by THOMAS KEIGHTLEY. 6 vols. London, 1864.

1871 seq. FURNESS.

SAMUEL A. TANNENBAUM: Textual errors in the Furness Variorum. In: MLN., vol. 45, 1930, pp. 510–14.

1893 seq. The Warwick Shakespeare. General editorship: C. H. HERFORD.
21 vols. London, 1893 seq.

The editors of the various plays are as follows: As, Ado by J. C. SMITH; Cor., Haml.,
Macb., Mids. by E. K. CHAMBERS; Cymb. by A. J. WYATT; I H. IV by F. W. MOOR-
MAN; 2 H. IV, Oth., R. II, Wint. by C. H. HERFORD; H. V, John by MOORE SMITH;
H. VIII, Lear by D. NICHOL SMITH; Caes., Tw. by A. D. INNES; Merch. by H. L.
WITHERS; R. III by GEORGE MACDONALD; Temp. by F. S. BOAS.

1904–7. William Shakespeare: Complete Works. Comedies, histories,
tragedies, poems and sonnets. Ed. by A. H. BULLEN. 10 vols. The Shakespeare Head Press, 1904–7. The Stratford Town Edition.

The concluding volume contains the following Essays: William Shakespeare: Memoir,
by HENRY DAVEY; Ben Jonson's Views on Shakespeare's Art, by J. J. JUSSERAND; On
the Influence of the Audience, by ROBERT BRIDGES; The Religion of Shakespeare, by
H. C. BEECHING; The Stage of the Globe, by E. K. CHAMBERS; The Sonnets, by H. C.
BEECHING; The Portraits of Shakespeare, by M. H. SPIELMANN; Notes on the Text, by
A. H. BULLEN.

1921 seq. QUILLER-COUCH and J. D. WILSON. (13) Tw. 1930. (14) Wint. 1931.
(15) Haml. 1933.

Cf. also: J. DOVER WILSON: Thirteen volumes of Shakespeare. A retrospect.
In: MLR., vol. 25, 1930, pp. 397–414.

SAMUEL A. TANNENBAUM: How not to edit Shakespeare. A review. In:
Phil. Quart., vol. 10, 1931, pp. 97–137.

(4) TEXTUAL CRITICISM

(*page 58*)

EDWARD HENRY SEYMOUR: Remarks critical, conjectural, and explanatory on
the plays of Shakespeare. 2 vols. London, 1805.

Annotations illustrative of the plays of Shakespeare by Johnson, Steevens,
Malone, Theobald, Warburton, Farmer, Heath, Pope, Hawkins, Hanmer,
Sir J. Reynolds, Percy, etc. In 2 vols. London, 1819.

Z. JACKSON: Shakespeare's genius justified: being restorations and illustrations
of 700 passages in Shakespeare's plays. London, 1819. (xvi, 470 pp.)

F. A. LEO: Die Delius'sche Kritik der von J. Payne Collier aufgefundenen alten
handschriftlichen Emendationen zum Shakespeare gewürdigt. Berlin, 1853.

SAMUEL BAILEY: On the received text of Shakespeare's dramatic writings and
its improvement. 2 vols. London, 1862, 1866.

KARL ELZE: Notes on Elizabethan dramatists with conjectural emendations of
the text. 3 Bde. Halle, 1880–6. ²1889 (in one vol., xii, 356 pp.)

LEON KELLNER: Erläuterungen und Textverbesserungen zu 14 Dramen Shakespeares. Aus d. Nachlass hrsg. v. WALTHER EBISCH. Leipzig, 1931. (xi,
354 S.) Rev.: Lbl. 54, 1933, Sp. 310–12, W. Fischer; RESt. 9, 1933, pp.
474–6, R. B. McKerrow; Rev. anglo-amér. 11, 1933/4, pp. 336–8, A. Koszul;
Bbl. 45, 1934, S. 103–7, Albert Eichler; Sh. Jb. 70, 1934, S. 138–9, Wolfg.
Keller; Engl. Studies, 14, 1932, S. 27–32, B. A. P. van Dam.

Plays explained: Mids., John, Merch., Wiv., Caes., Ado, As, Tw., Haml., Troil.,
Meas., Oth., Macb., Temp.

G. N. GIORDANO-ORSINI: Nuovi orientamenti della filologia shakespeariana. Firenze, 1932. (46 pp.) Rev.: Bbl. 45, 1934, S. 274-5, L. L. Schücking.

RONALD B. MCKERROW: The treatment of Shakespeare's text by his earlier editors, 1709-68. O.U.P., for Brit. Acad. 1933. (35 pp.)=Annual Shakespeare Lecture, 1933.

SAMUEL A. TANNENBAUM: Some emendations of Shakspere's text. In his Shaksperian scraps and other Elizabethan fragments. New York, 1933, pp. 87-117.

ARNOLD SCHRÖER: Shakespeareana. (Hamlet I. 2. 65, Othello I. 2. 23, Lear I. 4. 307). In: Anglia, Bd. 59, 1935, S. 385-90.

VI. SHAKESPEARE'S SOURCES, LITERARY INFLUENCES, AND CULTURAL RELATIONS

(1) GENERAL

(a) COLLECTED SOURCES OF SHAKESPEARE'S WORKS

(page 61)

The Shakespeare Classics. General editor SIR I. GOLLANCZ.
'The Troublesome Reign of King John', being the original of Shakespeare's 'Life and Death of King John'. Edited by F. J. FURNIVALL and JOHN MUNRO. 1913.
The sources of Hamlet. With an essay on the legend, by ISRAEL GOLLANCZ. 1926.

(b) GENERAL STUDIES

(page 62)

A. L. ATTWATER: Shakespeare's sources. In: A companion to Shakespeare studies. C.U.P., 1934, pp. 219-41.

(c) SHAKESPEARE'S READING AND BOOK-KNOWLEDGE

(page 62)

PETER WHALLEY: Enquiry into the learning of Shakespeare, with remarks on several passages of his plays. London, 1748. (84 pp.)

R. W. BABCOCK: The attitude toward Shakespeare's learning in the late 18th century. In: Phil. Quart., vol. 9, 1930, pp. 116-22.

Supplement: THE THOUGHT AND LEARNING OF SHAKESPEARE'S TIMES

(page 63)

ALICE WALKER: The reading of an Elizabethan. Some sources of the prose pamphlets of THOMAS LODGE. In: RESt., vol. 8, 1932, pp. 264-81.

LOUIS B. WRIGHT: Middle class culture in Elizabethan England. Chapel Hill, 1935. (xi, 733 pp.)

(d) WORKS ON XVIth-CENTURY TRANSLATIONS IN GENERAL

(*page* 63)

F. O. MATTHIESSEN: Translation, an Elizabethan art. Harv. Univ. Pr., 1931. (viii, 232 pp.) Rev.: TLS. June 11, 1931, p. 462; MLR. 27, 1932, pp. 88–90, Kathleen M. Lea; MLN. 47, 1932, pp. 479–80, George Coffin Taylor; JEGPh. 34, 1935, pp. 121–3, Jacob Zeitlin.

(2) SHAKESPEARE AND CLASSICAL LITERATURE

(a) GENERAL TREATISES

(*page* 64)

A. H. CRUICKSHANK: The classical attainments of Shakespeare. In: Winchester College Shakespeare Society. Noctes Shakespearianae. Ed. by C. H. HAWKINS. 1887.

ALBERT TESCH: Das Nachleben der Antike in Shakespeares Dramen. In: Wiener Blätter für d. Freunde der Antike, Bd. 7, 1930, H. 38.

WALTER F. SCHIRMER: Chaucer, Shakespeare und die Antike. In: Bibliothek Warburg. Vorträge, 1930–1. Leipzig, 1932, S. 83–102.

(b) ENGLISH TRANSLATIONS OF THE ANCIENT CLASSICS IN THE XVIth CENTURY

(*page* 64)

HENRY B. LATHROP: Translations from the classics into English, from Caxton to Chapman, 1477–1620. Madison, 1933 (350 pp.)=Univ. of Wisconsin Stud. in Lang. and Lit., No. 35. Rev.: MLR. 29, 1934, pp. 345–6, B. E. C. Davis; Bbl. 45, 1934, S. 356–61, Walter F. Schirmer; MLN. 50, 1935, pp. 195–8, Merritt Y. Hughes.

(c) INFLUENCE OF INDIVIDUAL LATIN CLASSICAL AUTHORS

(*page* 65)

EDGAR I. FRIPP: Shakespeare's use of Ovid's Metamorphoses. In his Shakespeare studies. O.U.P., 1930, pp. 98–128.

Plinius. T. W. BALDWIN: A note upon William Shakespeare's use of Pliny. In: Parrott Presentation Volume, 1935, pp. 157–82.

Seneca. RUDOLF FISCHER: Zur Kunstentwicklung der englischen Tragödie von ihren Anfängen bis zu Shakespeare. Strassburg, 1893. (xiii, 192 pp.)

Terentius. PAUL TSCHERNJAJEW: Shakespeare und Terenz. In: Anglia, Bd. 55, 1931, S. 282–95.

(d) INFLUENCE OF THE GREEK CLASSICAL AUTHORS

β. INDIVIDUAL GREEK AUTHORS

(*page* 67)

Homer. ADOLF BEKK: Shakespeare und Homer. Ein Beitrag zur Literatur und Bühne des englischen Dichters. Pest, 1865. (160 S.)

VINC. SAPIENZA: Shakespeare contro Omero. Milano, 1930. (151 pp.)

Plutarch. A. VOLLMER: Shakespeare und Plutarch. In: Arch., Bd. 77, 1887, S. 353–403 u. Bd. 78, S. 75–114, 215–70.

MARTHA HALE SHACKFORD: Plutarch in Renaissance England, with special reference to Shakespeare. Wellesley, 1929. (54 pp.)

Sophocles. HALL FRYE: Shakespeare and Sophocles. In the same author's Romance and tragedy. Boston, 1922, pp. 227–311.

FRIEDRICH DANNENBERG: Das Erbe Platons in England bis zur Bildung Lylys. Berlin, 1932. (246 S.)=Neue Forschung. H. 13. Rev.: Bbl. 44, 1933, S. 122–6, Fr. Krog.

(e) CLASSICAL MYTHOLOGY

(*page* 68)

DOUGLAS BUSH: Mythology and the Renaissance tradition in English poetry. Minneapolis, Univ. Minnesota Pr., 1932. (x, 360 pp.) Rev.: MLN. 48, 1933, pp. 261–3, Charles G. Osgood; JEGPh. 33, 1934, pp. 130–2, Warner G. Rice; Rev. anglo-amér. 11, 1934, pp. 445–7, Floris Delattre; MLR. 30, 1935, pp. 228–9, G. D. Willcock.

HENRY GIBBONS LOTSPEICH: Classical mythology in the poetry of Edmund Spenser. Princeton Univ. Pr., 1932. (x, 126 pp.) Rev.: JEGPh. 34, 1935, pp. 116–17, Clark S. Northup.

CHARLES W. LEMMI: The classic deities in Bacon. A study in mythological symbolism. Baltimore, 1933. (ix, 224 pp.) Rev.: Phil. Quart. 14, 1935, p. 188, Frederick M. Padelford.

(3) INFLUENCE OF CONTEMPORARY CONTINENTAL LITERATURE

(b) INFLUENCE OF ITALIAN LITERATURE

(a) GENERAL

(*page* 69)

SIDNEY LEE: Shakespeare and the Italian Renaissance. In his Elizabethan and other essays. Oxford, 1929, pp. 140–68.

(γ) INDIVIDUAL ITALIAN AUTHORS

(*page* 71)

Aretino. JOHN LOTHIAN: Shakespeare's knowledge of Aretino's plays. In: MLR., vol. 25, 1930, pp. 415–24.

Machiavelli. H. BECK: Machiavellismus in der Renaissance. Diss. Bonn, 1935. (45 S.)

Tasso. SIDNEY LEE: Tasso and Shakespeare's England. In his Elizabethan and other essays. Oxford, 1929, pp. 169–83.

(δ) ITALIAN CONDUCT BOOKS AND THE ENGLISH IDEAL OF A GENTLEMAN

(page 72)

BALDASSARE CASTIGLIONE: The book of the courtier. Englished by THOMAS HOBY, 1561. Ed. by WALTER ALEXANDER RALEIGH. London, 1900=Tudor Translations 23. Hoby's translation also published in: Everyman's Library, vol. 807. London, 1928. (xviii, 324 pp.)

A. W. REED: Chivalry and the idea of a gentleman. In: Chivalry. A series of studies to illustrate its historical significance and civilizing influence. Ed. by EDGAR PRESTAGE. London, 1928, pp. 207–28.

ALEXANDER CORBIN JUDSON: Spenser's theory of courtesy. In: PMLA., vol. 47, 1932, pp. 122–36.

AUGUST HOYLER: Gentleman-Ideal und Gentleman-Erziehung. Mit besonderer Berücksichtigung der englischen Renaissance. Leipzig, 1933. (xi, 224 S.) Rev.: Bbl. 45, 1934, S. 188–91, Georg Dost; Engl. Studies, 16, 1934, pp. 194–6, Paul Meissner.

JOHN E. MASON: Gentlefolk in the making. Studies in the history of English courtesy literature and related topics from 1531 to 1774. Philadelphia, 1935. (xiii, 393 pp.)

(c) INFLUENCE OF FRENCH LITERATURE

(β) INDIVIDUAL FRENCH AUTHORS

(page 73)

LEON KELLNER: Shakespeare und Montaigne. In: Dt. Rundschau, Jg. 36, 1910, S. 140–53.

SUSANNE TÜRCK: Shakespeare und Montaigne. Ein Beitrag zur Hamlet-Frage. Berlin, 1930. (v, 160 S.)=Neue Forschung. H. 8. Rev.: Bbl. 42, 1931, S. 124–6, H. Jantzen; N. Spr. 40, 1932, S. 106–8, W. Franz; Dt. Litztg. 53, 1932, Sp. 931–6, Herb. Schöffler; Engl. Studies, 14, 1932, pp. 220–4, H. de Groot; Lbl. 54, 1933, Sp. 17–19, Ernst A. Philippson; Neophilologus, 19, 1934, S. 128–9, H. de Groot.

RENÉ GALLAND: Montaigne et Shakespeare. Bordeaux, 1933. (41 pp.)

MAX DEUTSCHBEIN: Shakespeare's Kritik an Montaigne in 'As you like it'. In: Neuphilol. Monatsschr., Jg. 5, 1934, S. 369–85.

(d) INFLUENCE OF SPANISH LITERATURE

(β) INDIVIDUAL SPANISH AUTHORS

(page 74)

W. P. KER: Cervantes, Shakespeare, and the pastoral idea. In: A book of homage to Shakespeare, ed. by ISRAEL GOLLANCZ. London, 1916, pp. 49–51.

(e) INFLUENCE OF GERMAN LITERATURE
(β) INDIVIDUAL GERMAN AUTHORS
(page 75)

GOTTFRIED HÖFER: Die Bildung Jakob Ayrers. Leipzig, 1929. (vii, 96 S.)= Von deutscher Poeterey, Bd. 6. Rev.: JEGPh. 30, 1931, pp. 432–3, Neil C. Brooks.

(4) INFLUENCE OF ENGLISH NON-DRAMATIC LITERATURE
(page 75)

J. CHURTON COLLINS: Shakespeare and Holinshed. In his Studies in Shakespeare. London, 1904, pp. 241–76.

ALFRED HART: Shakespeare and the homilies, and other pieces of research into the Elizabethan drama. London, 1935. (262 pp.) Rev.: Bbl. 46, 1935, S. 112–16, Ph. Aronstein.

ALWIN THALER: Shakspere and Spenser. In: Sh. Assoc. Bull., vol. 10, 1935, pp. 192–211, and vol. 11, 1936, pp. 33–40.

(5) INFLUENCE OF CONTEMPORARY ENGLISH DRAMATISTS
(page 76)

WILHELM HORN: Das Volksschauspiel in Altengland. Vortrag. In: Mitt. der Schles. Ges. f. Volkskunde, Jg. 28, 1927, S. 1–9.

BONAMY DOBRÉE: Shakespeare and the drama of his time. In: A companion to Shakespeare studies. C.U.P., 1934, pp. 243–61.

(6) INFLUENCE OF FOLK-TALES, JEST-BOOKS, EMBLEM-BOOKS, ETC.
(page 78)

HERMAN OESTERLEY: Shakespeare's jest-book. A hundred mery talys, from the only perfect copy known. Ed., with introd. and notes. London, 1866. (xx, 162 pp.)

LUDWIG VOLKMANN: Bilderschriften der Renaissance. Leipzig, 1923.
Discusses the origin of the emblem fashion.

W. LANSDOWN GOLDSWORTHY: Shakespeare's heraldic emblems, their origin and meaning. London, 1928. (237 pp.)

MARIO PRAZ: Studi sul concettismo. Milano, 1934. (viii, 168 pp. and 75 plates).
Deals with emblem literature in its relation to the epigram and the concetto.

MARIO PRAZ: The English emblem literature. In: Engl. Studies, vol. 16, 1934, pp. 129–40.

VII. THE ART OF SHAKESPEARE

PART I. SHAKESPEARE'S LANGUAGE, VOCABULARY, PROSODY AND STYLE

(1) SHAKESPEARE'S LANGUAGE AND VOCABULARY

(*a*) SHAKESPEARE'S LANGUAGE IN GENERAL AND THE LANGUAGE OF HIS TIMES

(*page* 79)

G. D. WILLCOCK: Shakespeare and Elizabethan English. In: A companion to Shakespeare studies. C.U.P., 1934, pp. 117–36.

G. D. WILLCOCK: Shakespeare as critic of language. London, 1934. (30 pp.)= The Sh. Assoc.

WALTER F. SCHIRMER: Shakespeare und die Rhetorik. (Festvortrag.) In: Sh. Jb., Bd. 71, 1935, S. 11–31.

(*b*) PHONOLOGY, PRONUNCIATION, AND ORTHOGRAPHY

(*page* 81)

RICHARD GRANT WHITE: Memorandums of English pronunciation in the Elizabethan era. In his Works of William Shakespeare. Boston, 1861, vol. 12, pp. 411–38.

HARRY M. AYRES: The question of Shakspere's pronunciation. In: Shakespearian studies, ed. by B. MATTHEWS and A. H. THORNDIKE. New York, 1916, pp. 237–51.

F. G. BLANDFORD: Shakespeare's pronunciation. A transcription of 'Twelfth Night', act I, scene 5. Made for the Festival Theatre Company, Cambridge. Cambridge, 1927. (20 pp.)

(*e*) PUNCTUATION

(*page* 84)

EDWIN J. HOWARD: The printer and Elizabethan punctuation. In: Stud. in Phil., vol. 27, 1930, pp. 220–9.

PETER ALEXANDER: Shakespeare's punctuation. In: TLS. March 17, 1932, p. 195.

(*f*) THE VOCABULARY OF SHAKESPEARE AND HIS CONTEMPORARIES

(*a*) VOCABULARY IN GENERAL

(*page* 85)

MAX DEUTSCHBEIN: Die Bedeutungsentwicklung von *road* bei Shakespeare. In: Anglia, Bd. 59, 1935, S. 368–75.

W. S. MACKIE: Shakespeare's English, and how far it can be investigated with the help of the 'New English Dictionary'. In: MLR., vol. 31, 1936, pp. 1–10.

(δ) DICTIONARIES AND GLOSSARIES

(page 87)

J. M. JOST: Erklärendes Wörterbuch zu Shakespeares Plays. Berlin, 1840. (728 S.)

SWYNFEN JERVIS: A dictionary of the language of Shakespeare. London, 1868. (374 pp.)

CHARLES MACKAY: A glossary of obscure words and phrases in the writings of Shakespeare and his contemporaries. London, 1887.

(ε) CONCORDANCES

(page 88)

FRANCIS TWISS: A complete verbal index to the plays of Shakespeare, comprehending every substantive, adjective, verb, participle and adverb used by Shakespeare, with reference to every individual passage in which each word occurs. 2 vols. London, 1805.

W. H. DAVENPORT ADAMS: A concordance to the plays of Shakespeare. London, 1886. (495 pp.)

(ζ) DICTIONARIES OF QUOTATIONS

(page 89)

L. L. M. MARSDEN: Shakespearean quotations in every-day use. (A key to their source and context.) London, 1931. (160 pp.)

(2) SHAKESPEARE'S PROSODY

(a) GENERAL WORKS ON ENGLISH PROSODY

(page 89)

GEORGE YOUNG: An English prosody on inductive lines. C.U.P., 1928. (xiv, 296 pp.) Rev.: MLR. 24, 1929, pp. 488–9, B. E. C. Davis; JEGPh. 28, 1929, pp. 589–91, P. F. Baum.

(b) SHAKESPEARE'S PROSODY

(page 89)

E. A. ABBOTT: A Shakespearean grammar. London, 1873.
Cf. the chapter on prosody, pp. 328–429.

J. CHURTON COLLINS: The text and prosody of Shakespeare. In his Studies in Shakespeare. London, 1904, pp. 297–331.

DAVID LAURANCE CHAMBERS: The metre of Macbeth. Its relation to Shakespeare's earlier and later work. Princeton, 1903. (70 pp.) Rev.: Sh. Jb. 40, 1904, S. 300–1, A. Brandl.

FEDERICO GARLANDA: L'alliterazione nel dramma shakespeariano e nella poesia italiana. Roma, 1906. (xi, 77 pp.)

H. REIMER: Der Vers in Shakespeares nichtdramatischen Werken. Diss. Bonn, 1908. (60 S.)

E. K. CHAMBERS: The problem of chronology. In his William Shakespeare. A study of facts and problems. 1930, vol. 1, chap. 8, pp. 243–74, and Metrical tables, vol. 2, pp. 397–408 (=Appendix H).

CHARLES A. LANGWORTHY: A verse-sentence analysis of Shakespeare's plays. In: PMLA., vol. 46, 1931, pp. 738–51.

PHILIP W. TIMBERLAKE: The feminine ending in English blank verse. A study of its use by early writers in the measure and its development in the drama up to the year 1595. With full tables of percentages. Menasha, Wisc., 1931. (131 pp.)

WILHELM FRANZ: Shakespeares Blankvers, mit Nachträgen zu des Verfassers Sh.-Grammatik. Tübingen, 1932. (90 S.), ²1935. (104 S.) Rev.: Bbl. 44, 1933, S. 113–14, H. Jantzen.

(c) PROSODY OF SHAKESPEARE'S CONTEMPORARIES
(page 91)

PHILIP W. TIMBERLAKE: The feminine ending in English blank verse. Menasha, Wisc., 1931. (131 pp.) Rev.: Bbl. 44, 1933, S. 73–4, Karl Brunner.

(3) SHAKESPEARE'S LITERARY STYLE
(a) GENERAL WORKS ON SHAKESPEARE'S STYLE
(page 92)

MARTIN PERLE: Die Hyperbel und ihre Verwendung bei Shakespeare. Diss. Breslau, 1933. (49 S.)

(b) SIMILE AND METAPHOR
(page 93)

R. HOBURG: Einige Bilder und Personifikationen aus Shakspere. Progr. Husum, 1872. (26 S.)

MISS G. LATHAM: Shakespeare's metaphors in the comedies. In: Trans. New Sh. Soc., 1887–92, no. xviii.

CAROLINE F. E. SPURGEON: Leading motives in the imagery of Shakespeare's tragedies. London, for the Sh. Assoc., 1930. (46 pp.) Rev.: Bbl. 42, 1931, S. 50–1, H. Jantzen.

F. C. KOLBE: Shakespeare's way. A psychological study. London, 1930. (xii, 179 pp.) Rev.: TLS. Nov. 20, 1930, p. 958; Sh. Jb. 67, 1931, S. 86–7, Wolfg. Keller.

CAROLINE F. E. SPURGEON: Shakespeare's iterative imagery. O.U.P., 1931. (34 pp.)=Proc. Brit. Acad., vol. 17. (Annual Sh. Lecture.) Also in: Aspects of Shakespeare. O.U.P., 1933, pp. 255–86. Rev.: Bbl. 43, 1932, S. 117–20, Elise Deckner; RESt. 9, 1933, pp. 100–1, M. St. Clare Byrne.

T. R. HENN: Field sports in Shakespeare. In: Essays of the year 1933–1934. London, 1934.

CAROLINE F. E. SPURGEON: Shakespeare's imagery and what it tells us. C.U.P., 1935. (xvi, 408 pp.) Rev.: TLS. Oct. 3, 1935, p. 609.

WOLFGANG CLEMEN: Shakespeares Bilder, ihre Entwicklung und ihre Funktionen im dramatischen Werk. Mit einem Ausblick auf Bild und Gleichnis im elisabethanischen Zeitalter. Bonn, 1936. (339 S.)=Bonner Stud. z. engl. Philol., H. 27.

(c) SHAKESPEARE'S PROSE AND EUPHUISM

(a) SHAKESPEARE'S PROSE IN GENERAL

(page 94)

J. CHURTON COLLINS: Shakespeare as a prose writer. In his Studies in Shakespeare. London, 1904, pp. 180–208.

MAGDALENE KLEIN: Shakespeares dramatisches Formgesetz. Bindung von Vers und Prosa von Shakespeare bis zum deutschen Expressionismus. München, 1930. (83 S.)=Wortkunst. Untersuchungen zur Sprach- und Literaturgeschichte, hrsg. v. O. Walzel. N.F. 4. Rev.: Sh. Jb. 66, 1930, S. 218–20, W. Keller.

MAGDALENE KLEIN: Form und Aufbau der Tragödien Macbeth, Othello, Lear, Hamlet—ein Ausdruck des Wesens ihrer Handlungsträger. In: Anglia, Bd. 56, 1932, S. 69–100.

BERNHARD SCHERER: Vers und Prosa bei den jüngeren dramatischen Zeitgenossen Shakespeares. Ein Beitrag zum Studium der Formtechnik im englischen Renaissance-Drama. Diss. Münster, 1932. (61 S.)

(β) EUPHUISM

(page 95)

FRIEDRICH LANDMANN: Der Euphuismus, sein Wesen, seine Quelle, seine Geschichte. Diss. Giessen, 1881. (III S.) Also in English, entitled: Shakespeare and euphuism. In: Trans. New Sh. Soc., 1880–5, P. II, pp. 241–76.

CLARENCE GRIFFIN CHILD: John Lyly and euphuism. Erlangen und Leipzig, 1894. (xii, 123 S.)=Münchener Beiträge zur romanischen und engl. Philologie, H. 7. Rev.: E. St. 21, 1895, S. 117, Ph. Aronstein.

T. K. WHIPPLE: Isocrates and euphuism. In: MLR., vol. 11, 1916, pp. 15–27 and 129–35.

(d) PROVERBS, MAXIMS, RIDDLES, PUNS, ETC.

(a) PROVERBS AND MAXIMS

(aa) Collections

(page 96)

K. F. W. WANDER: Deutsches Sprichwörterlexikon. Leipzig, 1867–80.

WALTER GOTTSCHALK: Die sprichwörtlichen Redensarten der französischen Sprache. 2 Bde. Heidelberg, 1930. (x, 548 S.)

G. L. APPERSON: English proverbs and proverbial phrases. A historical dictionary. London and Toronto, 1929. (x, 721 pp.) Rev.: Mod. Phil. 29, 1931, pp. 242–4, Rich. Jente.

WILLIAM GEORGE SMITH: The Oxford dictionary of English proverbs. With introduction and index by Janet E. Heseltine. O.U.P., 1935. (xxviii, 644 pp.)

(bb) Treatises

(page 96)

KARL PFEFFER: Das elisabethanische Sprichwort in seiner Verwendung bei Ben Jonson. Diss. Giessen, 1933. (193 S.) Rev.: Bbl. 46, 1935, S. 143-6, Elise Deckner.

M. P. TILLEY and JAMES K. RAY: Proverbs and proverbial allusions in Marlowe. In: MLN., vol. 50, 1935, pp. 347-55.

(γ) POSIES

(page 97)

JOAN EVANS: English posies and posy rings. A catalogue with an introduction. London, 1931. (xxxii, 114 pp.) Rev.: RESt. 9, 1933, pp. 336-7, M. Channing Linthicum.

VIII. THE ART OF SHAKESPEARE

PART II. SHAKESPEARE'S DRAMATIC ART

(1) SHAKESPEARE'S CREATIVE FACULTIES

(page 98)

FRIEDRICH GUNDOLF: Shakespeare. Sein Wesen und Werk. 2 Bde. Berlin, 1928 und 1929. (467 und 453 S.) Rev.: Sh. Jb. 65, 1929, S. 189-90, W. Keller; Arch. 159, 1931, S. 222-30, H. Hecht.

J. W. MACKAIL: The approach to Shakespeare. O.U.P., 1930. (144 pp.)
An appreciation of Shakespeare as a creative artist, of his supremacy as a master of prose and verse.

MAX J. WOLFF: Shakespeares Stellung an der Grenze zweier Zeiten. In: GRM., Jg. 21, 1933, S. 425-38.

C. J. SISSON: The mythical sorrows of Shakespeare. London, for the Brit. Acad., 1934. (28 pp.) (Annual Sh. Lecture.)
Considers Shakespeare as constructive artist.

(2) SHAKESPEARE'S DRAMATIC TECHNIQUE

(a) GENERAL TREATISES ON SHAKESPEARE'S DRAMATIC TECHNIQUE

(a) TECHNIQUE OF THE DRAMA IN GENERAL

####### (page 99)

GUSTAV FREYTAG: Die Technik des Dramas. Leipzig, 1863, ¹¹1908. Engl. transl.: The technique of the drama. Chicago, 1895. Cf. WILHELM DILTHEY: Die Technik des Dramas. In: Sh. Jb., Bd. 69, 1933, S. 27-60.

(β) SHAKESPEARE'S TECHNIQUE IN GENERAL

(*page* 99)

FRIEDRICH BRINCKER: Poetik Shakespeares in den Römerdramen Coriolanus, Julius Caesar und Antony und Cleopatra. Diss. Münster, 1884. (160 S.)

F. C. KOLBE: Shakespeare's way. A psychological study. London, 1930. (xii, 179 pp.)

ELMER EDGAR STOLL: Shakespeare and the moderns: Corneille, Racine, Ibsen. In his Poets and playwrights. Minneapolis, 1930, pp. 55-138.

H. B. CHARLTON: Romanticism in Shakespearian comedy. Manch. Univ. Pr., 1930. (23 pp.)

H. B. CHARLTON: Shakespeare's recoil from romanticism. Manch. Univ. Pr., 1931. (27 pp.) Also in: Bull. John Rylands Libr., vol. 15, 1931, pp. 35-59.

MAGDALENE KLEIN: Form und Aufbau der Tragödien Macbeth, Othello, Lear, Hamlet. Ein Ausdruck des Wesens ihrer Handlungsträger. In: Anglia, Bd. 56, 1932, S. 69-100.

ELMER EDGAR STOLL: Art and artifice in Shakespeare. New York, 1933. (xv, 178 pp.) Rev.: JEGPh. 34, 1935, pp. 442-4, Harold N. Hillebrand; RESt. 11, 1935, pp. 482-3, G. B. Harrison; E. St. 70, 1936, S. 397-400, Eduard Eckhardt.

HARLEY GRANVILLE-BARKER: Shakespeare's dramatic art. In: A companion to Shakespeare studies. C.U.P., 1934, pp. 45-87.

RICHARD DAVID: The Janus of poets, being an essay on the dramatic value of Shakespeare's poetry, both good and bad. C.U.P., 1935. (176 pp.)

SIR JOHN SQUIRE: Shakespeare as a dramatist. London, 1935. (233 pp.) Rev.: The Book Soc.'s News, Sept. 1935, p. 8, Sylvia Lynd; TLS. Sept. 5, 1935, p. 548.

KARL OTTO BRAUN: Die Szenenführung in den Shakespeareschen Historien. Ein Vergleich mit Holinshed und Hall. Diss. Berlin, 1935. (viii, 176 S.)

ARTHUR C. SPRAGUE: Shakespeare and the audience. Cambridge, Mass., Harv. Univ. Pr., 1935. (xiii, 327 pp.)
Deals with the manner in which Shakespeare informs the audience of time and place, of beginnings and endings, of choruses, &c.

(γ) TECHNIQUE OF SHAKESPEARE'S CONTEMPORARIES

(*page* 101)

OLA ELIZABETH WINSLOW: Low comedy as a structural element in English drama from the beginnings to 1642. Diss. Chicago, 1926. (186 pp.) Rev.: Engl. Studies, 8, 1931, pp. 147-8, H. de Groot.

DORIS FENTON: The extra-dramatic moment in Elizabethan plays before 1616. Diss. Philadelphia, 1930. (125 pp.)

M. C. BRADBROOK: Themes and conventions of Elizabethan tragedy. C.U.P., 1935. (viii, 275 pp.) Rev.: MLR. 31, 1935, p. 78, G. B. Harrison.

(*b*) VARIOUS ASPECTS OF SHAKESPEARE'S DRAMATIC TECHNIQUE

(*a*) DEPENDENCE OF THE DRAMATIC FORM ON EXTERNAL INFLUENCES

(*aa*) *On Theatrical Conditions*

(*page* 102)

FERDINAND GREGORI: Shakespeare und die Schauspielkunst. In: Shakespeares Werke. Übertr. nach Schlegel-Tieck von MAX J. WOLFF. Berlin, 1926, Bd. 22, S. 241–305.

M. C. BRADBROOK: Elizabethan stage conditions. A study of their place in the interpretation of Shakespeare's plays. C.U.P., 1932. (149 pp.) Rev.: Rev. anglo-amér. 10, 1932, pp. 149–50, L. Cazamian.

(*bb*) *On Public Taste*

(*page* 102)

SIDNEY LEE: Shakespeare and the Elizabethan playgoer. In: Furnivall English Miscellany. Oxford, 1901, pp. 235–54.

J. DOVER WILSON: The Elizabethan Shakespeare. O.U.P., for the Brit. Acad., 1929. (27 pp.)

FREDSON THAYER BOWERS: The audience and the revenger of Elizabethan tragedy. In: Stud. in Phil., vol. 31, 1934, pp. 160–75.
Answers the question: 'How close were the sympathies of the Elizabethan audience with the revengeful motives and actions of the characters of the tragedy of revenge?'

MAX J. WOLFF: Shakespeare und sein Publikum. In: Sh. Jb., Bd. 71, 1935, S. 94–106.

(*γ*) ACT AND SCENE DIVISION

(*page* 104)

THORNTON SHIRLEY GRAVES: The 'act-time' in Elizabethan theatres. In: Stud. in Phil., vol. 12, 1915, pp. 103–34.

THOMAS M. RAYSOR: The aesthetic significance of Shakespeare's handling of time. In: Stud. in Phil., vol. 32, 1935, pp. 197–209.

(*δ*) SCENE TECHNIQUE

(*page* 105)

KARL OTTO BRAUN: Die Szenenführung in den Shakespeareschen Historien. Ein Vergleich mit Holinshed und Hall. Diss. Berlin. Würzburg, 1935. (176 S.)

M. C. BRADBROOK: Themes and conventions of Elizabethan tragedy. C.U.P., 1935. (275 pp.)

(*ε*) DEPICTION OF MILIEU AND INTERPRETATION OF NATURE

(*page* 105)

ALFRED NOYES: Shakespeare and the sea. In his Some aspects of modern poetry. London, 1924, pp. 191–213.

(ζ) USE OF MUSIC, SONGS, ACROBATICS, AND DANCES
(*page* 106)

FRANK A. PATTERSON: Shakspere and the medieval lyric. In: Shakespearian studies, ed. by B. MATTHEWS and A. H. THORNDIKE. New York, 1916, pp. 431–52.

WILLA MCCLUNG EVANS: Ben Jonson and Elizabethan music. Lancaster, Penn., 1929. (vi, 131 pp.)

ELISABETH BEUSCHER: Die Gesangseinlagen in den englischen Mysterien. Münster, 1930. (ix, 106 S.)

(θ) TYPICAL SCENES.—MOBS, GHOSTS, MADNESS, ETC.
(*page* 107)

LOUIS B. WRIGHT: Madmen as vaudeville performers on the Elizabethan stage. In: JEGPh., vol. 30, 1931, pp. 48–54.

P. V. KREIDER: The mechanics of disguise in Shakespeare's plays. In: The Sh. Assoc. Bull., vol. 9, 1934, pp. 167–80.

EBERHARD LUCIUS: Gerichtsszenen im älteren englischen Drama. Diss. Giessen, 1928. (59 S.)

JOHANNES HOFFMANN: Die Gerichtsszenen im englischen Drama von Shakespeare bis zur Schliessung der Theater (1642). Diss. Breslau, 1934. (85 S.)

(κ) MONOLOGUE, DIALOGUE, AND CHORUS
(*aa*) *Monologue*
(*page* 109)

ALOIS HINTERWALDNER: Der Monolog in Shakespeares Königsdramen. Ungedr. Diss. Innsbruck, 1931/2.

ELISABETH VOLLMANN: Ursprung und Entwicklung des Monologs bis zu seiner Entfaltung bei Shakespeare. Bonn, 1934. (168 S.)=Bonner Stud. z. engl. Philol., Heft 22. Rev.: Z.f.e.U. 33, 1934, S. 350–2, Wolfg. Keller; Dt. Litztg. 56, 1935, Sp. 508–10, P. Meissner; Sh. Jb. 71, 1935, S. 121–2, Wolfg. Keller.

(λ) PROLOGUE AND EPILOGUE
(*page* 110)

AUTREY NELL WILEY: Female prologues and epilogues in English plays. In: PMLA., vol. 48, 1933, pp. 1060–79.

(μ) ACTION AND CHARACTER
(*page* 110)

ELMER EDGAR STOLL: Art and artifice in Shakespeare. A study in dramatic contrast and illusion. C.U.P., 1933. (xv, 178 pp.) Rev.: TLS. Nov. 2, 1933, p. 746; Bbl. 45, 1934, S. 100–3, Ph. Aronstein; Sh. Jb. 70, 1934, S. 135–7, Wolfgang Keller; MLR. 29, 1934, pp. 449–50, C. J. Sisson; MLN. 50, 1935, pp. 200–2, T. M. Parrott.

(ν) ART OF CHARACTER DEPICTION

(aa) Problems of Character in General

(page 111)

BELLE SEDDON MATHESON: The invented personages in Shakespeare's plays. Diss. Univ. of Pennsylvania, 1932. (83 pp.) Rev.: Bbl. 45, 1934, S. 112–15, Elise Deckner; E. St. 70, 1936, S. 401–2, Eduard Eckhardt.

(bb) Particular Problems of Character

(page 111)

GEORG KRÄMER: Unmittelbare Selbstcharakterisierung und Charakterisierung durch Mithandelnde im englischen Drama der Renaissance. Diss. Breslau, 1930. (96 S.)

(cc) Individual Characters

(page 112)

THOMAS WHATELEY: Remarks on some of the characters of William Shakespeare. London, 1785. (82 pp.)

HEINRICH THEODOR RÖTSCHER: Shakespeare in seinen höchsten Charaktergebilden enthüllt und entwickelt. Dresden, 1864. (ix, 161 S.)

L. B. CAMPBELL: Shakespeare's tragic heroes. C.U.P., 1930. (xii, 248 pp.)

(dd) Character Types

(αα) Artisan and Professional Types

(page 112)

C. VAN DER SPEK: The church and the churchman in English dramatic literature before 1642. Diss. Amsterdam, 1930. (188 pp.)

J. DOVER WILSON: The schoolmaster in Shakespeare's plays. In: Royal Soc. of Literature. Essays by divers hands. New series, vol. 9. O.U.P., 1930.

AARON MICHAEL MYERS: Representation and misrepresentation of the Puritan in Elizabethan drama. Philadelphia, 1931. (151 pp.)

C. LIEBE: Der Arzt im elisabethanischen Drama. Diss. Halle, 1907. (50 S.)

ANNEMARIE PIETZKER: Der Kaufmann in der elisabethanischen Literatur. Diss. Freiburg i. Br., 1931. (76 S.)

MACLEOD YEARSLEY: Doctors in Elizabethan drama. London, 1933. (128 pp.)

LOUISE D. FRASURE: Shakespeare's constables. In: Anglia, Bd. 58, 1934, S. 384–91.

(ββ) Female Characters

(page 113)

LOUIS LEWES: Shakespeares Frauengestalten. Stuttgart, 1893. (xvi, 409 S.)

HANNS PASSMANN: Der Typus der Kurtisane im elisabethanischen Drama. Diss. München, 1926. (vii, 75 S.)

(γγ) Ghosts

(*page* 114)

[Anon.]: Ghost technique in Shakespeare. In: The Sh. Assoc. Bull., vol. 10, 1935, pp. 157–62.

(εε) The Melancholy Type

(*page* 114)

NICHOLAS BRETON: Melancholike humours. Ed. with an essay on Elizabethan melancholy by G. B. HARRISON. London, 1929. (vi, 89 pp.) Rev.: RESt. 6, 1930, pp. 355–6, G. D. Willcock.

(ζζ) Fools, Clowns, and the Devil

(*page* 115)

B. SWAIN: Fools and folly during the Middle Ages and the Renaissance. Columbia Univ. Pr., 1932. (242 pp.)= Studies in English and Comparative Literature.

ROBERT WITHINGTON: 'Vice' and 'parasite'. A note on the evolution of the Elizabethan villain. In: PMLA., vol. 49, 1934, pp. 743–51.

ROBERT H. HILL. A strange fraternity. In: Blackwood's Mag., vol. 225, 1934, pp. 725–44.
On fools and jesters in the Middle Ages and the Renaissance.

ENID WELSFORD: The fool. His social and literary history. London, 1935. Rev.: TLS. Oct. 10, 1935, p. 627.
Traces the history of the fool in legend and myth, in common life, at court, and on the stage: from classical times through the Middle Ages and the Renaissance.

(ηη) National Types

(*page* 115)

JOHN WESLEY HALES: Shakespeare and the Jews. In: Engl. Histor. Rev., vol. 9, 1894, pp. 652–61.

J. E. LLOYD: Shakespeare's Welshmen. In: A book of homage to Shakespeare, ed. by ISRAEL GOLLANCZ. London, 1916, pp. 280–3.

CUMBERLAND CLARK: Shakespeare and national character. A study of Shakespeare's knowledge and dramatic and literary use of the distinctive racial characteristics of the different peoples of the world. London, 1933. (308 pp.)

WILSON O. CLOUGH: The broken English of foreign characters of the Elizabethan stage. In: Phil. Quart., vol. 12, 1933, pp. 255–68.

(θθ) Social Types

(*page* 116)

FELIX E. SCHELLING: The common folk of Shakespeare. In: A book of homage to Shakespeare, ed. by ISRAEL GOLLANCZ. London, 1916, pp. 364–72.

JOHN W. DRAPER: Shakespeare's rustic servants. In: Sh. Jb., Bd. 69, 1933, S. 87–101.

MARGARET M. TOOLE: Shakespeare's courtiers. In: The Sh. Assoc. Bull., vol. 9, 1934, pp. 83–90.

DIETRICH TERGAU: Die sozialen Typen im Drama des englischen Mittelalters. Diss. Göttingen, 1931. (78 S.)

(*u*) Criminal Types
(*page* 116)

JUTTA HOLTZ: Abnorme Charaktere bei Shakespeare: Othello, Richard III., Macbeth. Diss. Tübingen, 1933. (47 S.)

(κκ) Various Types
(*page* 117)

AARON MICHAEL MYERS: Representation and misrepresentation of the Puritan in Elizabethan drama. Philadelphia, 1931 (151 pp.)

(ξ) THE LENGTH OF SHAKESPEARE'S PLAYS

EDWARD ROSE: Length of the acts in Shakspere's plays. In: New Shak. Soc. Trans., 1877–79, pp. 8–10.

L. L. SCHÜCKING: Zum Problem der Überlieferung des Hamlet-Textes. Leipzig, 1931. (42 S.)=Ber. Verh. Sächs. Akad. Wiss., Bd. 83, H. 4. Rev.: RESt. 8, 1932, pp. 228–31, W. W. Greg; Bbl. 43, 1932, S. 107–11, Ernst Groth; Lbl. 54, 1933, Sp. 19–20, Helene Richter; JEGPh. 31, 1932, pp. 597–9, Robert M. Smith.
How long was the average Elizabethan play? Why did Shakespeare write plays too long to be acted?

ALFRED HART: The number of lines in Shakespeare's plays. In: RESt., vol. 8, 1932, pp. 19–28.

ALFRED HART: The length of Elizabethan and Jacobean plays. In: RESt., vol. 8, 1932, pp. 139–54.

ALFRED HART: The time allotted for representation of Elizabethan and Jacobean plays. In: RESt., vol. 8, 1932, pp. 395–413.

ALFRED HART: Acting versions of Elizabethan plays. In: RESt., vol. 10, 1934, pp. 1–28.
The three last-named essays also in Alfred Hart's Shakespeare and the homilies. O.U.P., 1934, pp. 77–153.

(3) THE TRAGIC AND THE COMIC
(*page* 117)

W. J. M. STARKIE: Wit and humour in Shakespeare. In: A book of homage to Shakespeare, ed. by ISRAEL GOLLANCZ. London, 1916, pp. 212–26.

V. VENDYŠ: Úvodní kapitola ke studii o komice a patosu ve veselohrách Shakespearových. (Introductory chapter to a study of the comic and the pathetic in Shakespeare's comedies.) In: Studies in English by members of the English Seminar of the Charles Univ., Prague, vol. 1 (*c.* 1929).

ROBERT P. UTTER: 'Wise enough to play the fool.' In: Essays in criticism, by members of the Department of English. 2nd series. Univ. of California Pr., 1934, pp. 155-81.

MARGARET GALWAY: Flyting in Shakespeare's comedies. In: The Sh. Assoc. Bull., vol. 10, 1935, pp. 183-91.

PAUL V. KREIDER: Elizabethan comic character conventions as revealed in the comedies of George Chapman. Ann Arbor, 1935. (xii, 206 pp.)=Univ. of Michigan Publ., Lang. and Lit., 17.

(4) SYMBOLISM: ALLUSIONS TO PLACES AND TO CONTEMPORARY PERSONS AND EVENTS

(*page* 118)

LILIAN WINSTANLEY: Hamlet and the Scottish succession, being an examination of the relations of the play of Hamlet to the Scottish succession and the Essex conspiracy. C.U.P., 1921. (x, 188 pp.) Rev.: Sh. Jb. 58, 1922, S. 132-4, W. Keller; Bbl. 35, 1924, S. 2-6, B. Fehr.

LILIAN WINSTANLEY: Macbeth, King Lear, and contemporary history, being a study of the relations of the play of Macbeth to the personal history of James I, the Darnley murder, and the St. Bartholomew massacre, and also of King Lear as symbolic mythology. C.U.P., 1922. (viii, 228 pp.) Rev.: Sh. Jb. 58, 1922, S. 134-6, W. Keller; MLR. 18, 1923, pp. 209-13, C. H. Herford; Bbl. 35, 1924, S. 6-12, B. Fehr.

LILIAN WINSTANLEY: Othello as the tragedy of Italy, showing that Shakespeare's Italian contemporaries interpreted the story of the Moor and the Lady of Venice as symbolizing their country in the grip of Spain. London, 1924. (152 pp.) Rev.: Marzocco, 30, 1925, p. 45, G. S. Gargano.

EVELYN MAY ALBRIGHT: Shakespeare's Richard II, and the Essex conspiracy. In: PMLA., vol. 42, 1927, pp. 686-720.

EVELYN MAY ALBRIGHT: The folio version of 'Henry V' in relation to Shakespeare's times. In: PMLA., vol. 43, 1928, pp. 722-56.
She sees allusions to Essex in the passages in the Folio which are missing in the quartos.

PERCY ALLEN: Shakespeare and Chapman as topical dramatists. 1929.
Cf. TLS. Sept. 12, 1929, p. 704 (P. Allen) and Sept. 19, p. 723 (S. A. Ferguson).

B. M. WARD: Shakespeare and the Anglo-Spanish War. In: Rev. anglo-amér., vol. 6, 1929, pp. 297-311.

G. B. HARRISON: Shakespeare's topical significances. In: TLS. Nov. 13 and 20, 1930.

LESLIE HOTSON: Shakespeare versus Shallow. London, 1931. (376 pp.)

THOMAS WHITFIELD BALDWIN: William Shakespeare adapts a hanging. Princeton Univ. Pr., 1931. (202 pp.) Rev.: JEGPh. 31, 1932, pp. 429-33, Rob. M. Smith.

FREDERICK J. HARRIES: Shakespeare and the Scots. Edinburgh, 1932. (147 pp.)

G. B. HARRISON: Shakespeare at work, 1592-1603. London, 1933. (x, 326 pp.) Rev.: TLS. Oct. 5, 1933, p. 667.
Demonstrates the close relation of Shakespeare's plays to the events of the time.

G. B. HARRISON: The national background. In: A companion to Shakespeare studies. C.U.P., 1934, pp. 163-86.
Deals with the question of allusions.

PERCY ALLEN: The plays of Shakespeare and Chapman in relation to French history. London, 1933. (xv, 339 pp.) Rev.: TLS. Aug. 3, 1933, p. 522.

IX. SHAKESPEARE'S STAGE AND THE PRODUCTION OF HIS PLAYS

(1) THE THEATRE

(a) HISTORY OF THE ELIZABETHAN THEATRE

(β) GENERAL TREATISES

(*page* 120)

PERCY FITZGERALD: A new history of the English stage. 2 vols. London, 1882.

J. J. JUSSERAND: Les théâtres de Londres au temps de Shakespeare. In: La Revue de Paris, 9e année, t. 6, Paris, 1902, pp. 713-49.

E. K. CHAMBERS: The Elizabethan stage. 4 vols.

B. WHITE: An index to 'The Elizabethan stage' and 'William Shakespeare' by E. K. Chambers. Oxford, 1934. (vi, 162 pp.)

H. K. MORSE: Elizabethan pageantry. London, 1934. (128 pp.)

Le théâtre élizabéthain. In: Cahiers du Sud. Numéro spécial, juin/juillet. Marseille, 1933. (250 pp.) Cf. FLORIS DELATTRE: Le théâtre élizabéthain. A propos d'une publication récente. In: Rev. anglo-amér., vol. 11, 1934, pp. 385-409.

GEORGE WILLIAM SMALL: Shakspere's stage. In: The Sh. Assoc. Bull., vol. 10, 1935, pp. 31-5.

WILLIAM J. LAWRENCE: Those nut-cracking Elizabethans. Studies of the early theatre and drama. London, 1935. (xii, 212 pp.)
Fourteen essays, already previously published, but revised and rewritten.

WILLIAM J. LAWRENCE: Old theatre days and ways. London, 1935. Rev.: TLS. Jan. 11, 1936, p. 27.
Twenty-four single chapters in theatrical history.

(c) PUBLIC AND PRIVATE THEATRES

(a) PLAN AND SITUATION

(*page* 123)

J. ISAACS: Production and stage-management at the Blackfriars Theatre. London, 1933. (28 pp.)=Sh. Assoc. Pamphlet.

GERTRUD HILLE: Londoner Theaterbauten zur Zeit Shakespeares. (Mit einer Rekonstruktion des Fortuna-Theaters.) In: Sh. Jb., Jg. 66, 1930, S. 25-78.

(β) STAGING AND STAGE MACHINERY
(*page* 125)

WILLIAM J. LAWRENCE: Light and darkness in the Elizabethan theatre. In his The Elizabethan playhouse and other studies. 2nd series. Stratford-upon-Avon, 1913, pp. 1–22.

JOSEPH QUINCY ADAMS: Hamlet's 'Brave o'erhanging firmament'. In: MLN., vol. 30, 1915, pp. 70–2.
Deals with the painted firmament covering part of the stage.

WILLIAM J. LAWRENCE: The tragic carpet. In: The New Statesman and Nation. N.S., vol. 1, 1931, p. 284.
Deals with an eighteenth-century stage custom.

J. ISAACS: Production and stage-management at the Blackfriars Theatre. London, 1933. (28 pp.) Rev.: Bbl. 45, 1934, S. 117–18, W. Fischer.

GERTRUD ADRIAN: Die Bühnenanweisungen in den englischen Mysterien. Diss. Münster, 1931. (vi, 70 S.)

PETER WILHELM BIESTERFELDT: Die Oberbühne bei Marlowe. In: Arch., Bd. 160, 1931, S. 51–61.

E. LAUF: Die Bühnenanweisungen in den englischen Moralitäten und Inter-ludien bis 1570. Diss. Münster, 1932. (109 S.)

JOHANNES BEMMANN: Die Bühnenbeleuchtung vom geistlichen Spiel bis zur frühen Oper als Mittel künstlerischer Illusion. Diss. Leipzig, 1933.
Cf. in particular: iv, 3, *c*: England, pp. 129–36.

(2) THE ACTORS AND THEIR ART
(*b*) DRAMATIC COMPANIES AND THEIR PERFORMANCES
(*page* 128)

E. K. CHAMBERS: Performances of plays. In his William Shakespeare. A study of facts and problems. O.U.P., 1930, vol. 2, pp. 303–53 (=Appendix D).

C. J. SISSON: The theatres and companies. In: A companion to Shakespeare studies. London, 1934, pp. 9–43.

ROBERT BOIES SHARPE: The real war of the theaters. Shakespeare's fellows in rivalry with the Admiral's Men, 1594–1603. Repertories, devices, and types. Boston, 1935. (viii, 260 pp.)=The Mod. Lang. Assoc. of America. Monograph Series, 5. Rev.: MLR. 31, 1936, pp. 213–15, H. Harvey Wood.
Shows 'the differing literary policies of the two companies and their causes in differences of patronage and audience'.

(*c*) ENGLISH PLAYERS ON THE CONTINENT
(α) COLLECTIONS OF THEIR PLAYS AND GENERAL TREATISES
(*page* 129)

M. J. NORDSTRÖM: Friedrich Menius, l'aventureux professeur de Dorpat, et son rôle oublié dans l'histoire du drame des comédiens anglais. In: Samlaren, 1921.

ANNA BAESECKE: Das Schauspiel der englischen Komödianten in Deutschland, seine dramatische Form und seine Entwicklung. Halle, 1935. (154 S.)= Studien z. engl. Philol. H. 87.

(β) SPECIAL ESSAYS ON VISITS TO VARIOUS CITIES AND COUNTRIES
(*page* 130)

JOHANNES MEISSNER: Die englischen Komödianten in Österreich. Wien, 1884. (viii, 198 S.)=Beiträge z. Gesch. d. dt. Lit. u. d. geist. Lebens in Österreich, 4.

KARL TRAUTMANN: Englische Komödianten in Ulm (1594–1657). In: Arch. f. Lit. gesch., Jg. 13, 1885, S. 315–24.

J. CRÜGER: Englische Komödianten in Strassburg im Elsass. In: Arch. f. Lit. gesch., Jg. 15, 1887, S. 113–25.

A. DUNCKER: Landgraf Moritz von Hessen und die englischen Komödianten. In: Dt. Rundschau, Jg. 12, 1886, S. 260–75.

H. HARTLEB: Deutschlands erster Theaterbau. Eine Geschichte des Theaterlebens und der englischen Komödianten unter Landgraf Moritz dem Gelehrten von Hessen-Kassel. Berlin, 1936. (162 S.)

(d) INDIVIDUAL ACTORS
(*page* 130)

G. E. BENTLEY: Records of players in the Parish of St. Giles, Cripplegate. In: PMLA., vol. 44, 1929, pp. 789–826.

ROBERT BOIES SHARPE: James Hill, player. In: MLN., vol. 48, 1933, pp. 99–100.

[Anon.]: Will Kemp. In: Sh. Jb., Jg. 22, 1887, S. 255–64.

HENRY DAVID GRAY: The rôles of William Kemp. In: MLR., vol. 25, 1930, pp. 261–73. Cf. also: MLR., vol. 26, 1931, pp. 170–4.

(g) THE ART OF THE ACTOR IN THE TIME OF SHAKESPEARE

(α) GENERAL
(*page* 132)

ELISABETH LAUF: Die Bühnenanweisungen in den englischen Moralitäten und Interludien bis 1570. Diss. Münster, 1932. (xii, 109 S.)

(γ) COMMEDIA DELL'ARTE

(aa) *The Italian Improvised Comedy*
(*page* 133)

BENEDETTO CROCE: Sul significato storico e il valore artistico della commedia dell'arte. Nota letta all'Accad. d. scienz. morali e politiche d. Soc. Reale di Napoli. Vol. 52, 1929. (12 pp.) Rev.: Litbl. 51, 1930, Sp. 52–3, K. Vossler.

MAX J. WOLFF: Die Commedia dell'arte. In: GRM., Jg. 21, 1933, S. 307–18.

K. M. LEA: Italian popular comedy. A study in the commedia dell'arte, 1560–1620, with special reference to the English stage. 2 vols. O.U.P., 1934. (714 pp.) Rev.: RESt. 11, 1935, pp. 82–9, Alice Walker; MLR. 30, 1935, pp. 364–72, John Purves; Mod. Phil. 33, 1935, pp. 197–201, C. R. Baskervill.

(δ) DRAMATIC PLOTS (STAGE ABRIDGEMENTS)
(*page* 134)

W. W. GREG: Dramatic documents from the Elizabethan playhouses. Stage plots, actors' parts, prompt copies. 2 vols 1. Reproductions and transcripts. 2. Commentary. O.U.P., 1931. (plates; xiii, 378 pp.) Rev.: RESt. 8, 1932, pp. 219–28, W. J. Lawrence; Bbl. 43, 1932, S. 103–7, Walther Fischer; MLR. 28, 1933, pp. 95–8, E. K. Chambers; JEGPh. 32, 1933, pp. 609–13, Jos. Quincy Adams.

B. A. P. VAN DAM: A prompt-book text of 'The Alchemist' and its important lesson. In: Neophilologus, vol. 19, 1934, pp. 205–20.

X. LITERARY TASTE IN SHAKESPEARE'S TIME

(3) THE ELIZABETHAN THEATRE PUBLIC; POPULAR TASTE AND THE LITERARY TASTE OF THE PERIOD IN GENERAL
(*page* 138)

LOUIS B. WRIGHT: The Renaissance middle-class concern over learning. In: Phil. Quart., vol. 9, 1930, pp. 273–96.

LOUIS B. WRIGHT: The reading of Renaissance English women. In: Stud. in Phil., vol. 28, 1931, pp. 671–88. Also in: Royster Memorial Studies, 1931, pp. 139–56.

XI. AESTHETIC CRITICISM OF SHAKESPEARE

(1) XVIIth AND XVIIIth CENTURY CRITICISM
(*a*) SOURCES
(*page* 139)

GUSTAV WÜRTENBERG: Shakespeare in Deutschland. Bielefeld, 1931. (145 S.)= Velhagen und Klasings Deutsche Ausgaben, Bd. 265.

(*b*) TREATISES
(*page* 140)

A. KOBERSTEIN: Shakespeares allmähliches Bekanntwerden in Deutschland und Urteile über ihn bis zum Jahre 1773. In his Vermischte Aufsätze zur Literaturgeschichte. Leipzig, 1858.

HERTHA ISAACSEN: Der junge Herder und Shakespeare. Berlin, 1930. (103 S.)

ROBERT WITBECK BABCOCK: The genesis of Shakespeare idolatry (1766–99). A study in English criticism of the late 18th century. Chapel Hill: Univ. of North Carolina Pr., 1931. (xxviii, 307 pp.) Rev.: Sh. Jb. 67, 1931, S. 91–2,

W. Keller; JEGPh. 31, 1932, pp. 294-6, Tucker Brooke; Rev. anglo-amér. 10, 1932, pp. 150-1, Émile Legouis; Engl. Studies, 15, 1933, pp. 71-4, Fr. T. Wood.

AUGUSTUS RALLI: A history of Shakespearian criticism. 2 vols. London, 1932. (x, 566 and 582 pp.) Rev.: TLS. June 30, 1932, pp. 469-70; MLR. 28, 1933, pp. 98-101, Barry Garrad; Bbl. 44, 1933, S. 97-102, L. L. Schücking; RESt. 9, 1933, pp. 486-7, William S. Clark.
A compendious history of aesthetic opinion on Shakespeare from his own time to the end of 1925 in England, France, and Germany.

V. K. AYAPPAN PILLAI: Shakespeare criticism from the beginnings to 1765. London, 1933. (vi, 85 pp.)

HERBERT SPENCER ROBINSON: English Shakespearian criticism in the 18th century. New York, 1932. (x, 300 pp.)

T. S. ELIOT: Shakespearian criticism. 1. From Dryden to Coleridge. In: A companion to Shakespeare studies. C.U.P., 1934, pp. 287-99.

HEINZ WOHLERS: Der persönliche Gehalt in den Shakespeare-Noten Samuel Johnsons. Diss. Hamburg, 1934. (92 S.)

SISTER MARY JUSTINIAN WARPEHA: The effect of the Reformation on the English 18th century critics of Shakespeare (1765-1807). Diss. Washington, Catholic Univ. of America, 1934. (viii, 92 pp.)

(2) XIXth AND XXth CENTURY CRITICISM

(a) CRITICAL WORKS

(*page* 141)

WILLIAM HAZLITT: Characters of Shakespeare's plays. London, 1817.

R. W. BABCOCK: The direct influence of late 18th century Shakespeare criticism on Hazlitt and Coleridge. In: MLN., vol. 45, 1930, pp. 377-87.

GEORG SCHNÖCKELBORG: August Wilhelm Schlegels Einfluss auf William Hazlitt als Shakespeare-Kritiker. Diss. Münster, 1930 (Emsdetten i. Westf., 1931). (viii, 55 S.)

COLERIDGE'S Shakespearean criticism, ed. by THOMAS MIDDLETON RAYSOR. 2 vols. London, 1931. (lxi, 256 and 375 pp.) Rev.: TLS. June 11, 1931, p. 463; MLN. 47, 1932, pp. 113-16, A. E. Dodds; RESt. 8, 1932, pp. 235-8, Edith J. Morley; E. St. 67, 1933, S. 416-20, Cyril C. Barnard.

HIPPOLYTE TAINE: Shakspeare. In his Histoire de la littérature anglaise. Paris, 1863, ³1874. (T. 2, chap. 4, pp. 163-280.)

WILHELM KÖNIG: Shakespeare als Dichter, Weltweiser und Christ. Durch Erläuterung von vier seiner Dramen und eine Vergleichung mit Dante dargestellt. Leipzig, 1873. (392 S.) Rev.: Sh. Jb. 8, 1873, S. 355-6, Karl Elze.

LEO N. TOLSTOI: Shakespeare. Eine kritische Studie. Übers. von M. Enckhausen. Hannover, 1906. (148 S.)

46 *General*

Cf. also: EMILE FAGUET: Shakespeare au tribunal de Tolstoi. In the same author's Propos de théâtre. 5ᵉ série. Paris, 1910, pp. 63–78.

RUDOLF WASSENBERG: Tolstois Angriff auf Shakespeare. Ein Beitrag zur Charakterisierung östlichen und westlichen Schöpfertums. Diss. Bonn, 1935. (44 S.)

BENEDETTO CROCE: Shakespeare e la critica shakespeariana. In: La Critica. Anno 17, 1919, pp. 129–222.

MAX J. WOLFF: Shakespeares Schaffen. In: Shakespeares Werke. Übertr. nach Schlegel-Tieck von Max J. Wolff. Berlin, 1926, Bd. 22, S. 89–152.

G. F. BRADBY: Short studies in Shakespeare. London, 1929. (viii, 195 pp.) Rev.: Rev. anglo-amér. 7, 1930, pp. 548–9, A. Brulé.

ELMER EDGAR STOLL: Poets and playwrights: Shakespeare, Jonson, Spenser, Milton. Minneapolis, 1930. (304 pp.)
Contains: Cleopatra (pp. 1–30); Henry V (pp. 31–54); Shakespeare and the moderns (pp. 55–138).

G. WILSON KNIGHT: The wheel of fire. Essays in interpretation of Shakespeare's sombre tragedies. O.U.P., 1930. (xix, 296 pp.) Rev.: RESt. 7, 1931, pp. 468–9, Clare Byrne; Bbl. 42, 1931, S. 274–82, Ernst Groth; MLN. 48, 1933, pp. 119–21, Alwin Thaler.

J. W. MACKAIL: The approach to Shakespeare. Oxford, 1930. (144 pp.) Rev.: TLS. April 2, 1931, p. 267; Bbl. 43, 1932, S. 178–80, Elise Deckner.

G. WILSON KNIGHT: The imperial theme. O.U.P., 1931. (400 pp.) Rev.: TLS. Jan. 21, 1932, p. 40; Sh. Jb. 68, 1932, S. 159–60, Hans Hecht.

LOUIS GILLET: Shakespeare. Paris, 1931. (349 pp.)

G. WILSON KNIGHT: The Shakespearian tempest. O.U.P., 1932. (342 pp.) Rev.: Bbl. 44, 1933, S. 109–11, Ludwig Borinski.

HERMANN MÜLLER: Nebenher. Glossen zu Shakespeare. Chemnitz, 1932. (79 S.)

RANJEE G. SHAHANI: Shakespeare through Eastern eyes. London, 1932. (190 pp.)

JOHN DRINKWATER: Shakespeare. London, 1933. (118 pp.)

WOLF MEYER-ERLACH: Shakespeare, die Verkörperung nordischer Schöpferkraft. München, 1935. (63 S.)=Nordische Seher und Helden, Bd. 3.

JOHN SQUIRE: Shakespeare as a dramatist. London, 1935. (xi, 233 pp.)

(b) TREATISES DEALING WITH THE SHAKESPEARE CRITICISM OF THE XIXth AND XXth CENTURY

(*page* 146)

EDMOND SCHERER: Shakespeare et la critique. In his Études sur la littérature contemporaine. T. 6, Paris, 1882, pp. 137–50.

C. H. HERFORD: A sketch of recent Shakesperian investigation <1893–1923> London, n.d. (vii, 58 pp.)

LASCELLES ABERCROMBIE: A plea for the liberty of interpreting. O.U.P., 1930. (30 pp.)=Annual Sh. lecture of the Brit. Acad., 1930. Rev.: TLS. July 10, 1930, p. 571; Bbl. 42, 1931, S. 293-5, A. Eichler.

JOHN M. ROBERTSON: The state of Shakespeare study. A critical conspectus. London, 1931. (198 pp.) Rev.: TLS. May 28, 1931, p. 423; RESt. 8, 1932, pp. 362-3, U. M. Ellis-Fermor.

AUGUSTUS RALLI: A history of Shakespearian criticism. 2 vols. London, 1932. (x, 566 and 582 pp.)
A compendious history of aesthetic opinion on Shakespeare from his own time to the end of 1925 in England, France, and Germany.

GEORGES CONNES: État présent des études shakespeariennes. Paris, 1932. (116 pp.) Rev.: Engl. Studies, 16, 1934, pp. 34-6, J. Kooistra.

PAUL DE REUL: La 'désintégration' de Shakespeare. Bruxelles, 1932. (38 pp.)

L. C. KNIGHTS: How many children had Lady Macbeth? An essay in the theory and practice of Shakespeare criticism. Cambridge, 1933. (70 pp.)

HANS NEUHOF: Moderne Shakespearekritik. Paul Ernst. In: Sh. Jb., Bd. 70, 1934, S. 65-88.

J. ISAACS: Shakespearian criticism. II. From Coleridge to the present day. In: A companion to Shakespeare studies. C.U.P., 1934, pp. 300-4.

C. J. SISSON: The mythical sorrows of Shakespeare. O.U.P., 1934. (28 pp.)= Annual Sh. lecture.
A protest against the romantic interpretation of Shakespeare's plays.

Supplement: SHORT INTRODUCTIONS TO THE STUDY
OF SHAKESPEARE
(page 146)

RAYMOND M. ALDEN: A Shakespeare handbook. New York, 1925. (xvi, 240 pp.) Rev.: JEGPh. 22, 1923, pp. 294-8. Revised ed. by OSCAR JAMES CAMPBELL. New York, 1932. (xvi, 304 pp.)

JOHN BAILEY: Shakespeare. London, 1929. (xv, 280 pp.) Rev.: TLS. Oct. 17, 1929, p. 815.

HARDIN CRAIG: Shakespeare. A historical and critical study with annotated texts of 21 plays. Chicago, 1931. (1194 pp.) Rev.: MLN. 47, 1932, pp. 69-70, H. S.

LOGAN PEARSALL SMITH: On reading Shakespeare. London, 1933. (191 pp.)
Admirable reflections on different sides of Shakespeare's art from a modern standpoint.

A companion to Shakespeare studies, ed. by HARLEY GRANVILLE-BARKER and G. B. HARRISON. C.U.P., 1934. (408 pp.) Rev.: MLR. 30, 1935, pp. 75-80, Hazelton Spencer; Bbl. 46, 1935, S. 105-9, George Skillan.

THOMAS MARC PARROTT: William Shakespeare. A handbook. New York and O.U.P., 1934. (vi, 266 pp.)
With critical bibliography.

XII. SHAKESPEARE'S INFLUENCE THROUGH THE CENTURIES

(1) SHAKESPEARE'S INFLUENCE IN ENGLAND

(a) GENERAL

(page 148)

JAMES R. SUTHERLAND: Shakespeare's imitators in the 18th century. In: MLR., vol. 28, 1933, pp. 21–36.

GEORG FROHBERG: Das Fortleben des elisabethanischen Dramas im Zeitalter der Restauration. In: Sh. Jb., Bd. 69, 1933, S. 61–86.

ARTHUR E. DU BOIS: Shakespeare and the 19th century drama. In: Journ. of Engl. Lit. Hist., vol. 1, 1934, pp. 163–96.

(b) LITERARY ALLUSIONS TO SHAKESPEARE

(page 148)

INGLEBY—SMITH—FURNIVALL—MUNRO: The Shakspere allusion-book. Re-issued with a preface by SIR EDMUND CHAMBERS. 2 vols. O.U.P., 1932. (lxxxviii, 527 and x, 558 pp.) Rev.: TLS. June 30, 1932, pp. 469–70; RESt. 9, 1933, pp. 477–8, G. B. Harrison.

FRED. L. JONES: Echoes of Shakespeare in later Elizabethan drama. In: PMLA., vol. 45, 1930, pp. 791–803.

A. BRUCE BLACK and ROBERT METCALF SMITH: Shakespeare allusions and parallels. Bethlehem, Penn., 1931. (59 pp.)=Lehigh Univ. Publ., vol. 5, no. 3. The Inst. of Research, *circ.* no. 51, Studies in the Humanities, no. 8.

E. K. CHAMBERS: Contemporary allusions. In his William Shakespeare. A study of facts and problems. O.U.P., 1930, vol. 2, pp. 186–237 (=Appendix B).

MARIE SCHÜTT: Zwei Shakespeare-Anspielungen. [1614 and *c.* 1635.] In: Bbl., Bd. 44, 1933, S. 127.

(c) SHAKESPEARE'S SIGNIFICANCE FOR VARIOUS ENGLISH AUTHORS

(page 148)

B. J. MORSE: Mr. (James) Joyce and Shakespeare. In: E. St., Bd. 65, 1931, S. 367–81.

ANTON WÜLKER: Shakespeares Einfluss auf die dramatische Kunst von Nathaniel Lee. Diss. Münster, 1933. (v, 64 S.)

PHILIPP ARONSTEIN: Bernard Shaws Verhältnis zu Shakespeare. In: N. Spr., Bd. 41, 1933, S. 65–8.

ELFRIEDE PROBST: Der Einfluss Shakespeares auf die Stuart-Trilogie Swinburnes (Auszug). Diss. München, 1934. (48 S.)

JESSE M. STEIN: Horace Walpole and Shakespeare. In: Stud. in Phil., vol. 31, 1934, pp. 51–68.

(2) SHAKESPEARE'S INFLUENCE OUTSIDE ENGLAND

(a) AMERICA
(page 150)

KARL KNORTZ: An American Shakespeare-bibliography. Boston, 1876. (16 pp.)

KARL KNORTZ: Shakespeare in Amerika. Gera, 1882. (85 S.)

CLIFTON JOSEPH FURNESS: Walt Whitman's estimate of Shakespeare. In: Harvard Studies and Notes in philol. and literature, vol. 14, 1932, pp. 1-33.

(b) THE CONTINENT IN GENERAL
(page 150)

GIUSEPPE SCHIAVELLO: La fama dello Shakespeare nel secolo XVIII. Camerino, 1904. (185 pp.)

(c) THE LATIN COUNTRIES

(α) FRANCE

(bb) *Influence on Individual French Writers*
(page 151)

H. WYNN RICKEY: Musset shakespearien. Thèse, Bordeaux, 1932. (193 pp.)

GEORGES MOULY: Sardou et Shakespeare. In: Rev. de France, vol. 12, 1932, pp. 79-94.

JOSEPH BARETTI: Discours sur Shakespeare et monsieur de Voltaire. London, 1777.

MARY-MARGARET H. BARR: A bibliography of writings on Voltaire, 1825-1925. New York, 1929. (xxiii, 123 pp.)
One chapter deals with Voltaire and Shakespeare.

ROBERT W. BABCOCK: The English reaction against Voltaire's criticism of Shakespeare. In: Stud. in Phil., vol. 27, 1930, pp. 609-25.

(β) SPAIN
(page 151)

ALFONSO PAR: Contribución a la bibliografía española de Shakespeare, catálogo bibliográfico de la colección del autor. Barcelona, 1930. (140 pp.)

JUAN FEDERIGO MUNTADAS: Discurso sobre Shakspeare y Calderón. Madrid, 1849. (32 pp.)

ALFONSO PAR: Shakespeare en la literatura española. 2 vols. Madrid, 1935.

(γ) ITALY
(page 151)

LACY COLLISON-MORLEY: Shakespeare in Italy. Stratford-on-Avon, 1916. (180 pp.)

SIRO ATTILIO NULLI: Shakespeare in Italia. Milano, 1918. (245 pp.) Rev.: La Critica, 17, 1919, pp. 244-53, Benedetto Croce.

GUIDO FERRANDO: Shakespeare in Italy. In: The Sh. Assoc. Bull., vol. 5, 1930, pp. 157-68.

(d) GERMANY AND THE GERMANIC COUNTRIES

(a) GERMANY

(aa) *General Treatises*

(*page* 152)

AUGUST KOBERSTEIN: Shakespeares allmähliches Bekanntwerden in Deutschland und Urteile über ihn bis zum Jahre 1773. In his Vermischte Aufsätze zur Literaturgeschichte und Ästhetik. Leipzig, 1853, S. 163-221.

LUDWIG G. LEMCKE: Shakespeare in seinem Verhältnis zu Deutschland. Vortrag. Leipzig, 1864. (26 S.)

CLAAS HUGO HUMBERT: Molière, Shakespeare und die deutsche Kritik. Leipzig, 1869. (510 S.)

RODERICH BENEDIX: Die Shakespearomanie. Zur Abwehr. Stuttgart, 1873. (iv, 446 S.)

ADOLF BARTELS: Shakespeare und das englische Drama im 16. und 17. Jahrhundert. München, 1912. (104 S.)=S. A. aus der 'Einführung in die Weltliteratur'.

Shakespeare in Deutschland. Hrsg. von GUSTAV WÜRTENBERG. Bielefeld, 1931. (145 S.)
Reprint of source material up to the period of romanticism.

LAWRENCE MARSDEN PRICE: The reception of English literature in Germany. Berkeley, California, 1932. (vii, 596 pp.)
Cf. especially the 2nd part: Shakespeare in Germany.

MAX WUNDT: Shakespeare in der deutschen Philosophie. Vortrag. In: Sh. Jb., Bd. 70, 1934, S. 9-36.

HANS HECHT: Shakespeare in unserer Gegenwart. In: Sh. Jb., Bd. 70, 1934, S. 117-33.

FRITZ WÖLCKEN: Shakespeares Zeitgenossen in der deutschen Literatur. Berlin, 1929. (80 S.). Also in: Neue Forschung, Bd. 5. Rev.: Bbl. 43, 1932, S. 120-4, Ernst Groth.

(bb) *Shakespeare's Significance for Various German Authors*

(*page* 153)

[*Ulrich Bräker*]: Etwas über William Shakespeares Schauspiele, von einem armen ungelehrten Weltbürger, der das Glück genoss, ihn zu lesen. Mit Vorbemerkung von HERMANN TODSEN. Berlin, 1911. (xii, 180 S.)

Cf. HERMANN CONRAD: Ein Mann aus dem Volk über Shakespeare. In: Preuss. Jbb. 146, 1911, S. 444-65.

HEINRICH VOGELEY: Georg *Büchner* und Shakespeare. Diss. Marburg, 1934. (vi, 55 S.)

H. G. GÖPPERT: Paul *Ernst* und die Tragödie. Leipzig, 1932. (viii, 191 S.)= Form und Geist, 29. Rev.: Arch., Jg. 88, Bd. 164, 1933, S. 257-8, A. Brandl.

AUGUST WILHELM SCHLEGEL: Etwas über W. Shakespeare bei Gelegenheit 'W. Meisters'. In: Die Horen, Bd. 6, 1795-7, S. 57-112.

HERMANN ULRICI: Shakespeares dramatische Kunst und sein Verhältnis zu Calderon und Goethe. Halle, 1839, ³1870.

HERMANN ULRICI: Goethe und Schiller in ihrem Verhältnis zu Shakespeare. In his: Abhandlungen zur Kunstgeschichte als angewandte Ästhetik. Leipzig, 1876, S. 218-91.

JAKOB MINOR und AUGUST SAUER: 'Götz' und Shakespeare. In: Studien zur Goethe-Philologie. Wien, 1880, S. 237-99.

JAMES BOYD: Goethe's knowledge of English literature. Oxford, 1932. (xvii, 310 pp.) Rev.: MLR. 39, 1934, pp. 106-8, L. A. Willoughby; JEGPh. 33, 1934, pp. 584-90, L. M. Price.
The first chapter (80 pp.) deals with Goethe's relation to Shakespeare.

ERNST KEPPLER: *Gryphius* und Shakespeare. Diss. Tübingen, 1921. (123 S.)

ADOLF BARTELS: *Hebbel* und Shakespeare. (Vortrag.) Heide, 1933. 60 S.= Jahresgabe der Hebbelgemeinde, 1932.

HERTHA ISAACSEN: Der junge *Herder* und Shakespeare. Diss. Hamburg. Berlin, 1930. (103 S.)=Germanische Studien, H. 93.

THEODOR FRIEDRICH: Die 'Anmerkungen über das Theater' des Dichters Jakob Michael Reinhold *Lenz*. In: Probefahrten, Bd. 13, 1909. (145 S.)

GEORG WITKOWSKI: Aristoteles und Sh. in *Lessings* 'Hamburgischer Dramaturgie'. In: Euphorion, Bd. 2, 1895, S. 517-29.

ARTHUR BÖHTLINGK: Lessing und Shakespeare=Shakespeare und unsere Klassiker. Bd. 1. Leipzig, 1909. (303 S.)

RICHARD M. MEYER: Otto *Ludwigs* Shakespearestudium. In: Sh. Jb., Jg. 37, 1901, S. 59-84.

FRITZ RICHTER: Otto Ludwigs Trauerspielplan 'Tiberius Gracchus' und sein Zusammenhang mit den 'Sh.-Studien.' Breslau, 1935. (89 S.)=Sprache und Kultur der germ. und roman. Völker. B, 12. Rev.: Dt. Litztg., Jg. 56, 1935, Sp. 1786-90, Kurt Vogtherr.

HELENE KALLENBACH: *Platens* Beziehungen zu Shakespeare. In: Stud. zur vgl. Lit. gesch., Bd. 8, 1908, S. 449-69.

ADOLF SEEBASS: *Raabe* und Shakespeare. In: GRM., Jg. 22, 1934, S. 1-22.

ARTHUR BÖHTLINGK: *Schiller* und Shakespeare=Böhtlingk: Shakespeare und unsere Klassiker, Bd. 3. Leipzig, 1910. (xiv, 457 S.)

JULIUS PETERSEN: Schiller und Shakespeare. In: Euphorion, Jg. 32, 1931, S. 145-65.

PAUL STECK: *Schiller* und Shakespeare. Eine stilistische Untersuchung. In: Sh. Jb., Jg. 71, 1935, S. 32-77.

GUSTAV WIENINGER: *Schopenhauer* in seiner Stellung zu Shakespeare. In: Sh. Jb., Jg. 66, 1930, S. 169-81.

MAX KOCH: Ludwig *Tiecks* Stellung zu Shakespeare. Vortrag. In: Sh. Jb., Jg. 32, 1896, S. 330-47.

EDWIN H. ZEYDEL: Ludwig Tieck and England. Princeton Univ. Pr., 1931. (vii, 264 pp.)

(β) THE REMAINING GERMANIC COUNTRIES

(*page* 155)

A. PANNEVIS: Shakspere en de hedendaagsche Nederlandsche uitgaven en vertalingen zijner tooneelstukken. Kritische bijdrage tot de kennis van dichter en dichtkunst. Utrecht, 1863. (viii, 64 S.)

JOAN BULMAN: Strindberg and Shakespeare. Shakespeare's influence on Strindberg's historical drama. London, 1933. (224 pp.)

NILS MOLIN: Shakespeare och Sverige intill 1800—talets mitt. En översikt av hans inflytande. Göteborg, 1930. (iv, 308 S.) Rev.: MLR. 26, 1931, pp. 369-70, J. G. Robertson; RESt. 9, 1933, pp. 223-5, Herbert G. Wright; Revue de synthèse, 5, 1933, pp. 308-10, Paul van Tieghem.

MARTIN B. RUUD: An essay toward a history of Shakespeare in Denmark. Minneapolis, 1920=Research Publ. of the Univ. of Minnesota, Studies in lang. and literature, no. 8.

PAUL V. RUBOW: Shakespeare paa Dansk. Et Udsnit af den literære Smags Historie. Copenhagen, 1932. (110 S.)

R. PENNINK: Nederland en Shakespeare. Achttiende eeuw en vroege romantiek. The Hague, 1936. (xii, 304 S.)

(e) THE SLAVONIC COUNTRIES

(α) RUSSIA

(*page* 155)

ERNEST J. SIMMONS: English literature and culture in Russia (1553-1840). Harvard Univ. Pr., 1935. Rev.: TLS. Sept. 19, 1935, p. 577.
Has a chapter on Shakespeare's influence on Russia.

ERNEST J. SIMMONS: Catherine the Great and Shakespeare. In: PMLA., vol. 47, 1932, pp. 790-806.

ARNOLD EILOART: Shakspere and Tolstoy. London, 1909.

G. WILSON KNIGHT: Shakespeare and Tolstoy. O.U.P., 1934. (28 pp.)=Engl. Assoc. Pamphlet 88.

RUDOLF WASSENBERG: Tolstois Angriff auf Shakespeare. Ein Beitrag zur Charakterisierung östlichen und westlichen Schöpfertums. Diss. Bonn, 1935. (44 S.)

(f) HUNGARY

(*page* 156)

JÓZEF BAYER: Shakespeare drámái hazánkban. 2 vols. Budapest, 1909. (475 and 385 pp.)
A full record of Hungary's contributions to Shakespeare philology.

(g) OTHER COUNTRIES (NOT INCLUDED ABOVE)
(page 156)

MARCU BEZA: Shakespeare in Roumania. London, 1931. (56 pp.)

(3) ALTERATIONS AND ADAPTATIONS

(a) GENERAL TREATISES
(page 156)

GEORGE C. D. ODELL: Shakespeare from Betterton to Irving. 2 vols. London, 1921. (xiv, 456 and viii, 498 pp.)

ALLARDYCE NICOLL: A history of Restoration drama, 1660-1700. Cambridge, 1923. Chap. II, sect. VI: Adaptations of Shakespeare and of other Elizabethan dramatists (pp. 161-7).

R. W. BABCOCK: The attack of the late 18th century upon alterations of Shakespeare's plays. In: MLN., vol. 45, 1930, pp. 446-51.

MARTIN ELLEHAUGE: Engelsk bearbejdelse af Shakespeare i det 17. aarhundrede. In: Edda, 34, 1934, S. 417-36.

(b) VARIOUS ADAPTERS OF SHAKESPEARE
(page 157)

HAROLD CHILD: The Shakespearian productions of John Philip *Kemble*. London, 1935. (22 pp.)=The Sh. Association.

(4) TRANSLATIONS OF SHAKESPEARE

(a) GERMAN TRANSLATIONS

(α) GENERAL WORKS DEALING WITH GERMAN TRANSLATORS AND TRANSLATIONS
(page 158)

Die *Shakespeare-Literatur* in Deutschland. Vollständiger Catalog sämtlicher in Deutschland erschienenen Übersetzungen W. Shakespeares . . . aller bezüglichen Erläuterungs- u. Ergänzungsschriften. Von 1762 bis Ende 1851. Cassel, 1852. (44 S.)

HANS ROTHE: Der Kampf um Shakespeare. Ein Bericht. Leipzig, 1936. (105 S.)

(β) THE MOST IMPORTANT GERMAN TRANSLATIONS
(page 158)

Shakespears theatralische Werke. Aus dem Englischen übersetzt von WIELAND

H. PONGS: Wieland und Shakespeare. In: Festschr. zum 200. Geburtstag des Dichters Wieland, hrsg. v. d. Stadtgemeinde Biberach. Biberach, 1933.

Shakespeares dramatische Werke. Übersetzt von August Wilhelm von Schlegel und Ludwig Tieck. 12 Bde. Berlin, 1839-40.

W. SCHULZ: Der Anteil des Grafen Wolf Baudissin an der Shakespeare-Übersetzung Schlegel-Tiecks. In: Zs. f. dt. Philol., Jg. 59, 1934, S. 52-67.

H. V. LANGERMANN: Ein Brief des Grafen Wolf Baudissin über die Vollendung der Schlegel-Tieckschen Shakespeare-Übersetzung. In: Sh. Jb., Bd. 71, 1935, S. 107–9.

Shakespeares dramatische Werke, übers. von PH. KAUFMANN. T. 1–4. Berlin u. Stettin, 1830–6.

Shakespearedramen. Übers. von O. GILDEMEISTER.

KÄTHE STRICKER: Otto Gildemeister und Shakespeare. In: Sh. Jb., Bd. 68, 1932, S. 128–39.

Neue Shakespeare-Übersetzung von HANS ROTHE. München. Cf. HANS ROTHE: Gründe, die gegen eine Neuübersetzung Shakespeares sprechen. Leipzig, 1927. (14 S.) (Privatdruck.)

Shakespeare's Werke. Übertragen nach Schlegel-Tieck von MAX J. WOLFF. 22 Bde. Berlin, Wegweiserverlag, 1926.

(*b*) TRANSLATIONS INTO OTHER GERMANIC LANGUAGES
(*page* 162)

Shakespeare's dramatische Werken, vertaald en toegelicht door A. S. KOK. 7 Bde. Amsterdam, 1871–1880.
Prose translation.

De werken van William Shakespeare, vertaald door L. A. J. BURGERSDIJK. 12 Bde. Leiden, 1884–8. Rev.: Sh. Jb. 25, 1890, S. 294–6, G. V.

PAUL V. RUBOW: Shakespeare paa Dansk. Et Udsnit af den litteraere Smags Historie. København, 1932. (110 S.)

PAUL V. RUBOW: Studier over danske Shakespeare-oversaettelser. Foersom og Lembcke. In: Acta philologica scandinavica, Aarg. 8, 1933, 97–135.

(*c*) TRANSLATIONS INTO ROMANCE LANGUAGES
(*a*) FRENCH TRANSLATIONS
(*page* 162)

Shakespeare, traduit de l'anglois par LE TOURNEUR. 20 vols. Paris, 1776–82.

M. G. CUSHING: Pierre Le Tourneur. Columbia Univ. Pr., 1908. (xii, 318 pp.) Cf. 'The translator of Shakespeare'=pp. 154–252.

Œuvres complètes de Shakespeare. Traduction de M. GUIZOT. 8 vols. Paris, 1821.

Œuvres complètes de William Shakespeare. Traduction de M. GUIZOT. Nouv. édition revue, avec une étude sur Shakespeare, des notices sur chaque pièce et des notes. 8 vols. Paris, 1860–2.

(*β*) SPANISH AND PORTUGUESE TRANSLATIONS
(*page* 163)

Shakespeare: Obras completas. Con un estudio preliminar y notas críticas por Luis Astrana Marín. Madrid. (2130 pp.)

(γ) ITALIAN TRANSLATIONS

(*page* 163)

Teatro completo di Shakespeare, voltato in prosa italiana da CARLO RUSCONI.
6 vol. Torino, 1852–8. Edizione definitiva. 7 vol. Torino, 1928.

Opere di Shakespeare, trad. di GIULIO CARCANO. Prima edizione illustrata.
Vol. I–XII. Milano, 1875–82.

Shakespeare: Teatro completo. Nuova traduzione di DIEGO ANGELI. 40 vol.
Milano, 1925–34.

(5) SHAKESPEARE AND THE MODERN STAGE

(a) GENERAL DRAMATURGIC LITERATURE

(*page* 163)

PERCY FITZGERALD: Shakespearean representation, its laws and limits. London, 1908. (145 pp.) Rev.: Sh. Jb. 45, 1909, S. 353, R. Fischer.

WILHELM KOPP: Das Tragödienkostüm von Betterton bis Kemble in seiner
Entwicklung zur historischen Treue (1660–1817). Diss. Bonn, 1929. (99 S.
u. 74 Abb.)

HARLEY GRANVILLE-BARKER: Prefaces to Shakespeare. First series. London,
1927. (xl, 231 pp.) Second series. London, 1930. (xii, 345 pp.) Rev.: The
Sh. Assoc. Bull. 6, 1931, pp. 135–44, E. E. Stoll.

HARLEY GRANVILLE-BARKER: Associating with Shakespeare. London, for the
Sh. Assoc., 1932. (31 pp.) Rev.: Bbl. 44, 1933, S. 116–19, Ernst Groth.

MARTIN LUSERKE: Shakespeare und das heutige deutsche Laienspiel. In: Sh.
Jb., Bd. 69, 1933, S. 112–20.

(b) SHAKESPEARIAN ACTORS

(α) GENERAL WORKS

(*page* 165)

WILLIAM HAZLITT: A view of the English stage, or, a series of dramatic criticisms. London, 1818. Also in: Centenary Edition, ed. by P. P. HOWE.
London, 1930 seq., vol. 5, pp. 169–379.

(β) INDIVIDUAL SHAKESPEARIAN ACTORS

(*page* 165)

ARTHUR MURPHY: The life of David Garrick. 2 vols. London, 1801.

JOSEPH KNIGHT: David Garrick. London, 1894.

HELENE RICHTER: Kainz. Wien, 1931. (336 S. u. 16 Abb.) Rev.: Arch. 161,
1932, S. 107–8, A. Brandl; E. St. 67, 1932, S. 125–7, Albert Eichler.

HAROLD NEWCOMB HILLEBRAND: Edmund Kean. New York, Columbia Univ.
Pr. and O.U.P., 1933. (x, 388 pp.)

PERCY H. FITZGERALD: The Kembles. 2 vols. London, 1871.

NAOMI ROYDE-SMITH: The private life of Mrs. Siddons. London, 1933. (319 pp.) Rev.: TLS. May 4, 1933, p. 309.

ELLEN TERRY'S Memoirs. With preface, notes, and additional biographical chapters by C. ST. JOHN CRAIG. London, 1933. (xiii, 359 pp.) Rev.: TLS. July 6, 1933, p. 461.

(c) SHAKESPEARE PERFORMANCES

(α) GENERAL WORKS

(page 167)

ALBERT LUDWIG: Shakespeare und die ältere deutsche Bühne. In: Shakespeares Werke. Übertr. nach Schlegel-Tieck von MAX J. WOLFF. Berlin, 1926, Bd. 22, S. 307-78.

GEORG ALTMANN: Shakespeare auf der deutschen Bühne des 19. Jahrhunderts. Ibid., S. 379-441.

MONTY JACOBS: Shakespeare auf der modernen Bühne. Ibid., S. 443-57.

TORSTEN HECHT: Shakespeare und das Problem der Raumbühne. In: Sh. Jb., Bd. 69, 1933, S. 121-30.

HAROLD CHILD: Shakespeare in the theatre from the Restoration to the present time. In: A companion to Shakespeare studies. C.U.P., 1934, pp. 325-46.

(β) VARIOUS THEATRES

(page 167)

WERNER DEETJEN: Shakespeare-Aufführungen unter Goethes Leitung. Festvortrag. In: Sh. Jb., Bd. 68, 1932, S. 10-35.

M. C. DAY and J. C. TREWIN: The Shakespeare Memorial Theatre. With forewords by Sir Frank Benson and W. Bridges-Adams. London and Toronto, 1932. (269 pp.)

G. A. JELLICOE: The Shakespeare Memorial Theatre, Stratford-upon-Avon. London, 1933. (xi, 98 pp.)

(6) ILLUSTRATIONS TO SHAKESPEARE'S WORKS

(page 168)

BOYDELL'S Shakespeare gallery. A collection of prints from pictures painted for the purpose of illustrating the dramatic works of Shakespeare, by the most distinguished artists of Great Britain. 2 vols. London, 1803.

SYLVESTER and E. HARDING: The whole historical dramas of William Shakespeare, illustrated by an assemblage of 168 plates, comprising portraits of the royal, noble, and other persons mentioned, together with those of editors, commentators, and actors and views of castles, towns, &c., of the respective places referred to, with short biographical and topographical accounts. 2 vols. London, 1811.

Illustrations of Shakespeare, comprised in 230 vignette engravings by THOMPSON, from designs by THURSTON, adapted to all editions. London and Leipzig, 1826.

CHARLES HEATH: Shakespeares Frauenbilder. Eine Sammlung weiblicher Portraits zu den sämtlichen Schauspielen des Dichters. 15 Hefte. London und Berlin, 1836–8.

Neue Shakespeare-Gallerie. Die Mädchen und Frauen in Shakespeare's dramatischen Werken. Leipzig, 1848, ³1866.

Shakespeare-Gallerie. 36 Blätter in Stahlstichen. Gezeichnet von MAX ADAMO, HEINRICH HOFMANN, HANS MAKART, FRIEDRICH PECHT, FRITZ SCHWOENER, AUGUST und HEINRICH SPIESS. Mit erläut. Text von FRIEDRICH PECHT. Leipzig, ²1882. (368 S.)

W. VON KAULBACH: Shakespeare-Gallerie in Kupferstichen von den Professoren E. EICHENS, GONZENBACH, A. HOFFMANN, L. JACOBY und SCHÄFFER. Berlin. (8 Blätter.)

Shakespeare-Gallerie von C. V. PILOTY, F. PILOTY, A. LIEZEN-MAYER, GABRIEL MAX, ADOLF SCHMITZ, PAUL THUMANN, A. MENZEL, H. LOSSOW und E. GRÜTZNER. Berlin.

(7) MUSICAL SETTINGS OF SHAKESPEARE'S WORKS, SONGS, ETC.

(a) GENERAL TREATISES

(page 169)

ALFRED ROFFE: The handbook of Shakespearean music. Being an account of 350 pieces of music set to words taken from the plays and poems of Shakespeare, the compositions ranging from the Elizabethan age to the present time. London, 1878. (vi, 121 pp.)

ALBERT SCHÄFER: Historisches und systematisches Verzeichnis sämtlicher Tonwerke aus den Dramen Schillers, Goethes, Shakespeares, Kleists, Körners, usw. Leipzig, 1886. (vii, 192 S.)

LEOPOLD HIRSCHBERG: Shakespeares Lyrik in der deutschen Musik. In: Westermanns Monatshefte, Jg. 60, 1916, S. 262–8.

ALLWYN CHARLES KEYS: Les adaptations musicales de Shakespeare en France jusqu'en 1870. Thèse de Paris. Paris, 1933. (232 pp.) Rev.: Revue de synthèse, t. 5, 1933, pp. 307–8, Paul van Tieghem.

(d) OPERAS ON SHAKESPEARIAN SUBJECTS

(page 169)

W. BARCLAY SQUIRE: Shakespearian operas. In: A book of homage to Shakespeare, ed. by ISRAEL GOLLANCZ. London, 1916, pp. 75–83.

(8) PROSE VERSIONS OF SHAKESPEARE'S PLAYS

(page 169)

A. T. QUILLER-COUCH: Historical tales from Shakespeare. London, 1900. (xii, 368 pp.)

MARY MACLEOD: The Shakespeare story-book. With introd. by SIDNEY LEE. London, 1902. (xxi, 460 pp.)

THOMAS CARTER: Stories from Shakespeare, retold. London, 1910. (286 pp.)

HÉLÈNE ADELINE GUERBER: (1) Stories of Shakespeare's comedies. London, 1910. (viii, 336 pp.) (2) Stories of Shakespeare's tragedies. New York, 1911. (349 pp.) (3) Stories of Shakespeare's English history plays. New York, 1912. (315 pp.)

THOMAS CARTER: Shakespeare's stories of the English kings, retold. London, 1912. (284 pp.)

(9) TRAVESTIES OF SHAKESPEARE'S PLAYS
(*page* 170)

GUSTAVE FRÉJAVILLE: Les travestis de Shakespeare. Paris, 1930. (115 pp.)

(10) DICTIONARIES OF QUOTATIONS
(*page* 170)

AUGUST CORRODI: Shakespeare. Lebensweisheit aus seinen Werken gesammelt. Winterthur, 1863, ²1864. (xxix, 145 S.)

HERMANN MARGGRAFF: William Shakespeare als Lehrer der Menschheit. Lichtstrahlen aus seinen Werken. Leipzig, 1864. (xii, 235 S.)

C. E. R. ALBERTI: Shakespeare-Album. Des Dichters Welt- und Lebensanschauung, aus seinen Werken systematisch geordnet. Berlin, 1864. (xxiv, 200 S.)

W. A. AHNE: Shakespeare-Blüten als Festgabe zur 300-jährigen Gedächtnisfeier des grossen britischen Dichters. Prag, 1864. (ix, 172 S.)

FRIEDRICH KREYSSIG: Shakespeare-Anthologie. Hamburg, 1864. (xxiv, 316 S.)

C. W. STEARNS: The Shakespeare treasury of wisdom and knowledge. New York, 1869. (viii, 436 pp.)

F. A. LEO: Geflügelte Worte und volkstümlich gewordene Aussprüche aus Shakespeares dramatischen Werken. In: Sh. Jb., Jg. 27, 1892, S. 4–107.

SOPHIE METZER: Shakespeare-Gedanken. Berlin, 1929. (191 S.)

(11) SHAKESPEARIAN SOCIETIES AND THEIR PUBLICATIONS
(*page* 170)

The Shakespeare Association Pamphlets. O.U.P., 1917 seq.:

12. C. J SISSON: Shakespeare in India. Popular adaptations on the Bombay stage. 1926. (26 pp.)

13. T. S. ELIOT: Shakespeare and the stoicism of Seneca. 1927. (17 pp.)

14. EDMUND BLUNDEN: Shakespeare's significances. 1928. (18 pp.)

15. CAROLINE SPURGEON: Leading motives in the imagery of Shakespeare's tragedies. 1930. (46 pp.)

16. H. GRANVILLE-BARKER: Associating with Shakespeare. 1931. (31 pp.)

17. J. ISAACS: Production and stage-management at the Blackfriars Theatre. 1933. (28 pp.)

18. G. D. WILLCOCK: Shakespeare as critic of language. 1934. (30 pp.)

The Shakespeare Association Facsimiles. A series of rare texts illustrating life and thought in Shakespeare's England, under the general editorship of G. B. HARRISON.

1. A dialogue concerning witches and witchcraftes, 1593. By GEORGE GIFFORD. Introd. by BEATRICE WHITE.

2. *Skialetheia;* or a shadow of truth in certaine epigrams and satyres, 1598. By EVERARD GUILPIN. Introd. by G. B. HARRISON.

3. A health to the gentlemanly profession of serving-men, 1598. By I. M. Introd. by A. V. JUDGES.

4. Vicissitudo rerum, 1600. By JOHN NORDEN. Introd. by D. C. COLLINS.

5. A short treatise of hunting, 1591. By THOMAS COCKAINE. Introd. by W. R. HALLIDAY. 1932. (xxii, 28 pp. and 8 illustr.)

6. Paradoxes of defence, 1599. By GEORGE SILVER. Introd. by J. DOVER WILSON. 1933. (xx, 82 pp. and 3 illustr.)

7. Present remedies against the plague, 1603, and Orders . . . to be executed in time of plague, 1592. Introd. by W. P. BARRETT. 1933. (xx, 28 pp.)

8. An almanack and prognostication for the year 1598, made by Thomas Buckminster. Introd. by EUSTACE F. BOSANQUET. 1935.

9. Battle of Nieuport, 1600. Introd. by D. C. COLLINS. 1935.

10. The life and death of Gamaliel Ratsey. Introd. by S. H. ATKINS. 1935.

The Bulletin of the Shakespeare Association of Japan. Waseda Univ., Tokio, 1930 seq.

(12) SHAKESPEARE AS A HERO IN LITERATURE

(a) DRAMA

(*page* 172)

MAX HECKER: Shakespeares Bild im Spiegel deutscher Dichtung. Vortrag. In: Sh. Jb., Bd. 68, 1932, S. 36–55.

FRANK HARRIS: Shakespeare and his love. A play in 4 acts and an epilogue. London, 1910. (96 pp.)

CHARLES WILLIAMS: A myth of Shakespeare. O.U.P., 1929. (146 pp.)

H. H. HAY: As Shakespeare was. A drama. London, 1931. (192 pp.)

(b) NOVEL

(*page* 172)

EDUARD STUCKEN: Im Schatten Shakespeares. Ein Roman. Berlin, 1929. (574 S.)

CAROLA OMAN: The best of his family. London, 1933. (407 pp.) Rev.: TLS. Sept. 21, 1933, p. 627.

C. LONGWORTH-CHAMBRUN: Mon grand ami Shakespeare. Souvenirs de John Lacy, comédien du roi, reconstitués. Paris, 1934. (iv, 307 pp.)

(13) SHAKESPEARE IN THE SCHOOLS AND UNIVERSITIES

(*page* 173)

FRIEDRICH PERLE: Die Auswahl der Shakespeare-Lektüre. In: Lehrproben u. Lehrgänge, Heft 13, 1887, S. 26–37.

WILHELM MÜNCH: Shakespeare-Lektüre auf deutschen Schulen. In: Sh. Jb., Jg. 38, 1902, S. 118–43.

ÉMILE HOVELAQUE: Comment faire connaître Shakespeare aux petits Français. In: A book of homage to Shakespeare, ed. by ISRAEL GOLLANCZ. London, 1916, pp. 392–8.

A. LÜDER: Shakespeare in den oberen Klassen des Realgymnasiums. In: N. Spr., Bd. 18, 1910, S. 129–44.

ARNO SCHNEIDER: Schulausgaben der Shakespeare-Dramen. In: E. St., Bd. 50, 1916–17, S. 164–88.

HENRY W. SIMON: The reading of Shakespeare in American schools and colleges. New York, 1933. (169 pp.)

WALTER HÜBNER: Shakespeare. In his: Die englische Dichtung in der Schule. Leipzig, 1934, S. 31–82.

J. GELHARD: Shakespeare in der deutschen höheren Schule. In: N. Spr., Jg. 43, 1935, S. 174–82.

MAGDALENE KLEIN: Shakespeares dramatisches Formgesetz in seiner Bedeutung für die Schule. In: Neuphil. Mschr., Jg. 6, 1935, S. 487–98.

XIII. CIVILIZATION IN SHAKESPEARE'S ENGLAND

(1) GENERAL WORKS

(*page* 173)

THOMAS PLATTERS des Jüngeren Englandfahrt im Jahre 1599. Hrsg. von HANS HECHT. Halle, 1929. (xi, 181 S.) Rev.: MLR. 24, 1929, pp. 468–9, G. C. Moore Smith; Sh. Jb. 65, 1929, S. 206–7, W. Keller; Bbl. 40, 1929, S. 117–23, S. B. Liljegren; Arch. 157, 1930, S. 110–11, K. Brunner.

CONYERS READ: Bibliography of British history. Tudor period, 1485–1603. Oxford, 1933. (492 pp.)

S. R. GARDINER: History of England, 1603–1642. 2 vols. London, 1893.

A. F. POLLARD: The history of England from the accession of Edward VI to the death of Elizabeth (1547–1603). London, 1923=The Political Hist. of England, vol. 6.
With detailed bibliography.

E. P. CHEYNEY: History of England from the defeat of the Armada to the death of Elizabeth, with an account of English institutions during the late 16th and early 17th century. 2 vols. New York, 1926. (viii, 589 pp.)

G. B. HARRISON: An Elizabethan journal. Being a record of those things most talked of during the years 1591-4. London, 1928. (xxiv, 430 pp.) The same: A second Elizabethan journal (1595-98). London, 1931. (xii, 400 pp.) The same: A last Elizabethan journal (1599-1603). London, 1933. (vii, 387 pp.) Rev.: TLS. Sept. 7, 1933, p. 589; MLR. 29, 1934, pp. 450-1, E. K. Chambers.
Day-by-day record of events in the age of Shakespeare.

J. E. NEALE: Queen Elizabeth. London, 1934. (402 pp.) Rev.: TLS. Feb. 8, 1934, p. 89.

EDITH HUMMEL: Grundzüge des englischen Charakters im Zeitalter der Königin Elisabeth, dargestellt aus der Seeliteratur dieser Zeit. Diss. Bonn, 1934. (59 S.)

(2) THE CHURCH AND THE MARPRELATE CONTROVERSY

(a) GENERAL WORKS ON THE STATE OF THE CHURCH

(page 175)

CLAUDE JENKINS: The church and religion in the age of Shakespeare. In: The Quart. Journ. of the Histor. Assoc., vol. 15, 1930, no. 59. (pp. 199-212.)

W. K. JORDAN: The development of religious toleration in England from the beginning of the Reformation to the death of Queen Elizabeth. London, 1932. (490 pp.) Rev.: TLS. June 9, 1932, p. 418.

GEORGE T. BUCKLEY: Atheism in the English Renaissance. Chicago Univ. Pr., 1932. (163 pp.) Rev.: E. St. 68, 1933, S. 256-8, Friedrich Brie.

(3) POLITICAL, SOCIAL, AND ECONOMIC CONDITIONS

(a) GENERAL WORKS

(page 176)

H. L. POWELL: History of the people of England: the Tudors and Stuarts. London, 1930. (viii, 424 pp.)

(b) ECONOMIC CONDITIONS

(page 176)

W. S. DAVIS: Life in Elizabethan days. A picture of a typical English community at the end of the 16th century. New York, 1930. (xii, 376 pp.)

(c) THE SOCIAL CLASSES

(page 177)

THEODOR VATKE: Der Gallant in Shakespeares London. In: Arch., Bd. 82, 1889, S. 303-6.

LUCIEN WOLFF: Jews in Elizabethan England. In: Trans. of the Jewish Hist. Soc. of England, 1924-7. London, 1929. (xi, pp. 1-91). Rev.: TLS. Jan. 10, 1929, p. 27.

(d) ROGUES AND VAGABONDS

(*page* 177)

The Elizabethan underworld: A collection of Tudor and early Stuart tracts and ballads telling of the lives and misdoings of vagabonds, thieves, rogues, and cozeners, and giving some account of the operation of the criminal law. The text prepared, with notes and an introd. by A. V. JUDGES. London, 1930. (lxiv, 543 pp.)

(4) THE ARTS

(*page* 177)

TH. VATKE: Gärten und Gartenkunst in Shakespeares England. In: Arch., Bd. 77, 1887, S. 85–102.

WILLIAM CHAPPELL: Popular music of the olden time. A collection of ancient songs, ballads, and dance tunes, illustrative of the national music of England. With short introductions to the different reigns and notices of the airs from writers of the 16th and 17th centuries. Also a short account of the minstrels. 2 vols. London [1856–9].

P. A. SCHOLES: The Puritans and music in England and New England. London, 1934. (xxii, 428 pp.)

(5) SCIENCE AND PEDAGOGY

(b) PEDAGOGY

(*page* 178)

A. M. STOWE: English grammar schools in the reign of Elizabeth. New York, 1908. (200 pp.)

L. B. WRIGHT: The Renaissance middle-class concern over learning. In: Phil. Quart., vol. 9, 1930, pp. 273–96.

NORMAN WOOD: The Reformation and English education. A study of the influence of religious uniformity on English education in the 16th century. London, 1931. (xiii, 365 pp.)

GEORGE A. PLIMPTON: The education of Shakespeare, illustrated from the schoolbooks in use in his time. O.U.P., 1933. (ix, 140 pp.) Rev.: MLR. 29, 1934, pp. 195–6, C. J. Sisson; Bbl. 46, 1935, S. 109–11, A. Szogs.

J. HOWARD BROWN: Elizabethan schooldays. An account of the English grammar schools in the second half of the 16th century. Oxford, 1934. (173 pp.)

(6) OTHER ASPECTS OF ELIZABETHAN CIVILIZATION

(a) FOLKLORE

(*page* 179)

MINOR WHITE LATHAM: The Elizabethan fairies, the fairies of folklore and the fairies of Shakespeare. New York, 1930. (viii, 313 pp.) Rev.: TLS. April 23, 1931, p. 322; RESt., vol. 8, 1932, pp. 102–3, M. A. Murray. With detailed bibliography.

J. HARVEY BLOOM: Folklore, old customs, and superstitions in Shakespeare's land. London, 1930. (168 pp.)

Handwörterbuch des deutschen Aberglaubens, hrsg. von HANNS BÄCHTOLD-STÄUBLI. Berlin, 1927 seq.

(b) DOMESTIC LIFE
(*page* 179)

C. HOLLYBAND and P. ERONDELL: The Elizabethan home, discovered in two dialogues. Ed. by M. ST. C. BYRNE. London, 1930. (xvi, 124 pp.)

CUMBERLAND CLARK: Shakespeare and home life. London, 1935.

(f) COSTUMES
(*page* 180)

IRIS BROOKE: English costume in the age of Elizabeth. The 16th century. London, 1933. (87 pp.)

H. K. MORSE: Elizabethan pageantry. A pictorial survey of costume and its commentators, from *c.* 1560–1620. London, The Studio, 1934. (128 pp.)
Contains 82 illustrations and a glossary of terms relating to Elizabethan dresses.

(g) LONDON AND STRATFORD
(a) LONDON
(*page* 180)

W. H. HUDSON: London life in Shakespeare's time. In his Idle hours in a library. San Francisco, 1898, pp. 1–62.

(l) GREAT ELIZABETHANS
(*page* 181)

CHARLOTTE CARMICHAEL STOPES: The life of Henry, third Earl of Southampton, Shakespeare's patron. C.U.P., 1922. (544 pp.)

MARIE SCHÜTT: Die englische Biographik der Tudor-Zeit. Hamburg, 1930. (162 S.)=Britannica. H. I. Rev.: RESt. 7, 1931, pp. 345–7, G. C. Moore Smith; Arch. 160, 1931, S. 121–2, A. Brandl; Rev. anglo-amér. 10, 1933, pp. 433–5, A. Koszul; E. St. 70, 1935, S. 275–80, H. Ch. Matthes.

DONALD A. STAUFFER: English biography before 1700. Cambridge, Mass., and London, 1930. (379 pp.) Rev.: MLR. 26, 1931, pp. 204–5, G. Kitchin; TLS. Dec. 11, 1930, p. 1061; RESt. 8, 1932, pp. 108–10, E. C. Batho; Litbl. 53, 1932, Sp. 317–19, Marie Schütt; E. St. 70, 1935, S. 280–5, H. Ch. Matthes.
With detailed bibliography.

FRANCES A. YATES: John Florio. The life of an Italian in Shakespeare's England. C.U.P., 1934. (364 pp.) Rev.: Rev. de litt. comp. 15, 1935, pp. 361–3, Lucien Cattan; RESt. 11, 1935, pp. 347–51, Alice Walker; MLR. 30, 1935, pp. 522–4, J. Dover Wilson; Sh. Jb. 71, 1935, S. 127–9, Wolfgang Keller; Arch. 168, 1935, S. 251, A. Brandl; MLN. 51, 1936, pp. 266–7, Merritt Y. Hughes.

The Great Tudors, ed. by KATHARINE GARVIN. London, 1935. (xxxi, 658 pp.)

CONTENTS: Francis *Bacon* by H. C. O'NEILL (pp. 625-40), Richard *Burbage* by SIR NIGEL PLAYFAIR (pp. 611-24), William Cecil, Lord *Burghley* by HILAIRE BELLOC (pp. 507-20), Edmund *Campion* by CHRISTOPHER HOLLIS (pp. 325-40), John *Colet* by JOHN BELL (pp. 35-52), Thomas *Cranmer* by R. ELLIS ROBERTS (pp. 217-38), Thomas *Cromwell* by DAVID MATHEW (pp. 131-44), The *Earl of Essex* by A. L. ROWSE (pp. 551-64), Sir Francis *Drake* by A. P. NEWTON (pp. 491-506), *Queen Elizabeth* by G. B. HARRISON (pp. 251-66), John *Fisher* by DOUGLAS WOODRUFF (pp. 85-100), John *Foxe* by HUGH MASSINGHAM (pp. 377-94), Sir Humphrey *Gilbert* by PETER FLEMING (pp. 341-60), Sir Richard *Grenville* by J. A. WILLIAMSON (pp. 431-48), Sir Thomas *Gresham* by R. H. MOTTRAM (pp. 309-24), Sir John *Hawkins* by PHILIP LINDSAY (pp. 461-74), *Henry VII* by C. H. WILLIAMS (pp. 1-20), *Henry VIII* by A. F. POLLARD (pp. 21-34), Richard *Hooker* by CHR. MORRIS (pp. 537-50), Ben *Jonson* by ENID GLEN (pp. 641-58), Robert *Kett* by ROBERT RANDALL (pp. 163-82), John *Knox* by CHARLES L. WARR (pp. 267-90), Hugh *Latimer* by BRIAN LUNN (pp. 201-16), John *Lyly* by H. J. MASSINGHAM (pp. 565-80), Christopher *Marlowe* by ALFRED NOYES (pp. 449-60), *Queen Mary I* by M. ST. CLARE BYRNE (pp. 183-200), *Mary Queen of Scots* by MARJORIE BOWEN (pp. 395-414), Sir Thomas *More* by R. W. CHAMBERS (pp. 101-16), Matthew *Parker* by M. THEODORA STEAD (pp. 291-308), Cardinal *Pole* by HAROLD CHILD (pp. 239-50), Sir Walter *Raleigh* by WYNYARD BROWNE (pp. 595-610), William *Shakespeare* by A. W. POLLARD and J. DOVER WILSON (pp. 581-94), Sir Philip *Sidney* by C. HENRY WARREN (pp. 361-76), John *Skelton* by W. H. AUDEN (pp. 53-68), Edmund *Spenser* by W. L. RENWICK (pp. 521-36), William *Tyndale* by A. W. REED (pp. 117-30), Sir Francis *Walsingham* by CONYERS READ (pp. 415-30), Peter *Wentworth* by HUGH ROSS WILLIAMSON (pp. 475-90), Cardinal *Wolsey* by E. P. CHEYNEY (pp. 69-84), Sir Thomas *Wyatt* by PAUL CHADBURN (pp. 145-62).

EDWARD THOMPSON: Sir Walter Raleigh, the last of the Elizabethans. London, 1935. (xvi, 388 pp.)

XIV. THE SHAKESPEARE-BACON CONTROVERSY AND SIMILAR THEORIES

(1) THE SHAKESPEARE-BACON CONTROVERSY

(*page* 182)

Deutsche Baconiana. Zeitschrift für Bacon-Shakespeare-Forschung. Jg. 1, Frankfurt a. M. 1930.

EDWIN BORMANN: Neue Shakespeare-Enthüllungen. Heft 1, 2. Leipzig, 1895. (71 und 106 S.)

H. HÄFKER: Was sagt Shakespeare? Die Selbstbekenntnisse des Dichters in seinen Sonetten. Ein Beitrag zur Shakespeare-Bacon Frage. Berlin, 1896. (138 S.)

J. CHURTON COLLINS: The Bacon-Shakespeare mania. In his Studies in Shakespeare. London, 1904, pp. 332-69.

KARL BLEIBTREU: Die Lösung der Shakespeare-Frage. Ein neue Theorie. Leipzig, 1907. (174 S.)

CHARLES CRAWFORD: The Bacon-Shakespeare question. In his Collectanea. 2nd ser. Stratford-on-Avon, 1907, pp. 64-147.

H. A. W. SPECKMAN: Francis Bacon is William Shakespeare. Ontcijferd uit

Bacon's Geheimschrift in zijn eigen Werk 'The advancement of learning' en uit de werken van William Shakespeare. Arnhem, 1916. (80 S.)

ALFRED VON WEBER-EBENHOFF: Bacon-Shakespeare-Cervantes. Zur Kritik der Shakespeare- und Cervantes-Feiern. Wien, 1917. (ix, 433 S.)

LUDWIG MATHY: Die Entwicklung der Bacon-Forschung 1848–1930. In: Deutsche Baconiana, Jg. I, 1930, S. 1–20.

E. LANDAU: Das Shakespeare-Mysterium. Eine charakterologische Untersuchung. Berlin, 1930. (237 S.)

KARL WANSCHURA: Die Sonette Shakespeares von Franz Bacon geschrieben. Wien, 1930. (40 S.) Rev.: Litbl. 53, 1932, Sp. 20–3, Albert Eichler.

CAROLINE F. E. SPURGEON: The use of imagery by Shakespeare and Bacon. In: RESt., vol. 9, 1933, pp. 385–96.
Points out that, as regards the proportions of the subject-matter of the images they respectively use, the difference between Shakespeare and Bacon is very marked.

(2) LITERATURE CONCERNING BACON AND BEARING ON THE SHAKESPEARE-BACON QUESTION
(page 185)

M. STURT: Francis Bacon. A biography. London, 1932. (xvi, 246 pp.)

(4) THE OXFORD THEORY
(page 186)

GEORGE FRISBEE: Edward de Vere. A great Elizabethan. London, 1932. (x, 145 pp.)

———

PERCY ALLEN: The case for Edward de Vere, 17th Earl of Oxford, as 'William Shakespeare'. London, 1930. (xi, 400 pp.)

MONTAGU W. DOUGLAS: The Earl of Oxford as 'Shakespeare'. An outline of the case. London, 1932. (172 pp.)

PERCY ALLEN: The Oxford-Shakespeare case corroborated. London, 1932. (ix, 341 pp.)

PERCY ALLEN: The life story of Edward de Vere as 'William Shakespeare'. London, 1932. (xv, 386 pp.) Rev.: TLS. June 23, 1932, p. 462.

GERALD PHILLIPS: The tragic story of 'Shakespeare', disclosed in the sonnets, and the life of Edward de Vere, 17th Earl of Oxford. London, 1932. (x, 236 pp.) Rev.: TLS. June 23, 1932, p. 462.

GEORGES CONNES: Encore cinq ans de travaux oxfordiens. In: Rev. anglo-amér., vol. II, 1933/4, pp. 193–207.

M. W. DOUGLAS: Lord Oxford was Shakespeare. London, 1935. (192 pp.)

(5) OTHER THEORIES

(*page* 186)

C. DEMBLON: Lord Rutland est Shakespeare. Le plus grand des mystères dévoilé. Shaxper de Stratford hors cause. Paris, 1912. (viii, 560 pp.)

PETER ALVOR: Eine neue Shakespeare-Biographie. Würzburg, 1930. (xii, 275 S.)

Alvor considers Sir Charles Blount, 8th Lord Mountjoy (1563–1606), the author of Shakespeare's plays.

PETER ALVOR: Die Shakespeare-Frage und das Ben Jonson-Problem. Würzburg, 1930. (97 S.)

Francis Bacon = the author of Ben Jonson's plays.

KARL SCHNEIDER: Neues Zeugnis für Rutland-Shakespeare. Mit einer Darstellung der Gründe und der Geschichte der Shakespeare-Frage. Berlin, 1932. (232 S.)

B. THE WORKS OF SHAKESPEARE EXAMINED INDIVIDUALLY

I. CHRONOLOGY OF THE DRAMAS

(*page* 187)

CHARLES BATHURST: Remarks on the difference in Shakespeare's versification in different periods of his life. London, 1857. (218 pp.)

E. K. CHAMBERS: The problem of chronology. In his William Shakespeare. A study of facts and problems. O.U.P., 1930, vol. I, chap. viii, pp. 243–74.

ROBERT ADGER LAW: On the dating of Shakspere's plays. In: The Sh. Assoc. Bull., vol. 11, 1936, pp. 46–51.

II. THE INDIVIDUAL DRAMAS

INTRODUCTION: *GENERAL TREATISES DEALING WITH THE VARIOUS TYPES OF DRAMA*

(b) ROMAN PLAYS

(*page* 189)

JOHN W. DRAPER: The realism of Shakespeare's Roman plays. In: Stud. in Phil., vol. 30, 1933, pp. 208–24.

(c) HISTORICAL PLAYS

(*page* 189)

EDUARD WILHELM SIEVERS: Shakespeares zweiter mittelalterlicher Dramen-Zyklus. Berlin, 1896. (xxiii, 256 S.) Rev.: Sh. Jb. 32, 1896, S. 321–3, P. Hartmann; Dt. Litztg. 17, 1896, Sp. 878–80, R. Fischer.

GIUSEPPE COSENTINO: I drammi storici inglesi di Shakespeare. Bologna, 1907. (260 pp.)

C. L. KINGSFORD: Fifteenth-century history in Shakespeare's plays. In his Prejudice and promise in 15th-century England. O.U.P., 1925, pp. 1–21.

JOHANNES SCHLAF: Komposition zweier Shakespearescher Dramenserien. In: Sh. Jb., Bd. 68, 1932, S. 80–6.

(d) COMEDY

(*page* 190)

GIUSEPPE COSENTINO: Le commedie di Shakespeare. Bologna, 1906. (255 pp.)

H. B. CHARLTON: Romanticism in Shakespearian comedy. In: Bull. John Rylands Libr., vol. 14, 1930, pp. 340–60.

WILLIAM WITHERLE LAWRENCE: Shakespeare's problem comedies. New York, 1931. (xi, 259 pp.) Rev.: TLS. July 16, 1931, pp. 554–5; JEGPh. 30, 1931, pp. 420–3, S. A. Tannenbaum; MLR. 27, 1932, pp. 216–18, Charles J.

Sisson; Bbl. 43, 1932, S. 111–13, Ph. Aronstein; MLN. 47, 1932, pp. 402–4, Hazelton Spencer; Engl. Studies, 18, 1936, pp. 81–3, A. G. van Kranendonk.
Deals with Shakespeare's moral principles in All's, Meas., Troil., and Cymb.

ALFRED YOUNG FISHER: An introduction to the study of Shakespearean comedy. 1st part. Thèse Dijon, 1931. (xix, 209 pp.)

JOHN W. DRAPER: Mistaken identity in Shakespeare's comedies. In: Rev. anglo-amér., vol. 11, 1933/4, pp. 289–97.

(d*) ROMANTIC PLAYS

(*page* 190)

EMILIE PFEIFFER: Shakespeares und Tiecks Märchendramen. Diss. Bonn, 1933. (85 S.)=Mnemosyne. Heft 13. Rev.: Sh. Jb. 71, 1935, S. 123–5. Wolfg. Keller.
Comparison of Tieck's 'Volksbuchdramen' (Blaubart, Genoveva, Oktavian) with Shakespeare's Mids., Wint., Cymb., Temp.

TITUS ANDRONICUS

(*page* 191)

(1) THE TEXT

The Bankside Shakespeare. Vol. 7: Titus Andronicus [parallel impression of Q 1600 and F]. Ed. by APPLETON MORGAN. New York, 1890. (235 pp.)

R. B. MCKERROW: A note on Titus Andronicus. In: Libr., vol. 15, 1934, pp. 49–53.

(2) LITERARY GENESIS

J. CHURTON COLLINS: Shakespearean paradoxes. In his Studies in Shakespeare. London, 1904, pp. 96–126.
Supposes Shakespeare to be the sole author of Tit.

C. F. TUCKER BROOKE: Titus Andronicus and Shakespeare. In: MLN., vol. 34, 1919, pp. 32–6.

LOVE'S LABOUR'S LOST

(*page* 193)

(2) LITERARY GENESIS

JOSEPH DE PEROTT: Eine spanische Parallele zu 'Love's Labour's Lost'. In: Sh. Jb., Jg. 44, 1908, S. 151–3.

JOHN PHELPS: Father Parsons in Shakespeare. In: Arch. 133, 1915, S. 66–86.

RUPERT TAYLOR: The date of 'Love's Labour's Lost'. New York, Columbia Univ. Pr., 1932. (x, 134 pp.) Rev.: MLN. 48, 1933, pp. 117–18, Austin K. Gray.
Assumes as date some time about the middle of 1596.

EVA LEE CLARK: The satirical comedy 'Love's Labour's Lost'. A study. New York, 1933. (188 pp.)

FRED SORENSEN: 'The Masque of the Muscovites' in Love's Labour's Lost. In: MLN., vol. 50, 1935, pp. 499–501.

DANIEL C. BOUGHNER: Don Armado as a gallant. In: Revue anglo-amér., vol. 13, 1935, pp. 18–28.

(2*) MISCELLANEOUS TREATISES

R. G. MOULTON: On the humour of 'Love's Labour's Lost' and 'As You Like It'. In: Trans. New Sh. Soc., 1887–92, no. xii.

THE COMEDY OF ERRORS
(page 194)
(1*) THE TEXT

SAMUEL A. TANNENBAUM: Notes on 'The Comedy of Errors'. In: Sh. Jb., Bd. 68, 1932, S. 103–24.

(1) LITERARY GENESIS

W. CLAUS: Über die Menächmen des Plautus und ihre Nachbildung, besonders durch Shakespeare. Progr. Stettin, 1861. (48 S.)

A. FRITZ: Die Menaechmi des Plautus und die Comedy of Errors des Shakespeare in ihrem Verhältnisse als Original und nachahmende Bearbeitung. Progr. Pisino, 1874. (31 S.)

PAUL WISLICENUS: Zwei neuentdeckte Shakespeare-Quellen. In: Sh. Jb., Jg. 14, 1879, S. 87–96.

JOH. GROENE: Zwei neu entdeckte Quellen zu Shakespeare's Komödie der Irrungen. In: Sh. Jb., Jg. 29/30, 1894, S. 281–7.

KARL ROEDER: Menechmi und Amphitruo im englischen Drama bis zur Restauration, 1661. Diss. Leipzig, 1904. (84 S.)
Cf. especially chap. III: Shakespeare's Anteil an den Menechmen und am Amphitruo, pp. 28–36.

ERMA M. GILL: The plot-structure of 'The Comedy of Errors' in relation to its sources. In: Univ. of Texas Studies in English, no. 10, 1930, pp. 13–65.

THOMAS WHITFIELD BALDWIN: William Shakespeare adapts a hanging. Princeton Univ. Pr., 1931. (202 pp.) Rev.: JEGPh. 31, 1932, pp. 429–33, Rob. M. Smith.

(2) DRAMATIC ART

H. B. CHARLTON: Shakespeare's recoil from romanticism. Manch. Univ. Pr., 1931. (27 pp.)=Repr. from: The John Rylands Libr. Bull., vol. 15, 1931.

(3) SUBSEQUENT HISTORY OF THE DRAMA

MARIANNE LABINSKI: Shakespeares Komödie der Irrungen. Das Werk und seine Gestaltung auf der Bühne. Teildruck. Diss. Breslau, 1934. (99 S.)

THE TWO GENTLEMEN OF VERONA
(page 195)
(1) LITERARY GENESIS

GREGOR SARRAZIN: Shakespeare in Mailand? In: Sh. Jb., Jg. 46, 1910, S. 114–17.

JULIA GRACE WALES: Shakespeare's use of English and foreign elements in the setting of The Two Gentlemen of Verona. In: Trans. Wisconsin Acad., vol. 27, 1932, pp. 85–125.

(2) DRAMATIC ART

H. B. CHARLTON: Romanticism in Shakespearian comedy. Manch. Univ. Pr., 1930. (23 pp.)

SAMUEL ASA SMALL: The ending of The Two Gentlemen of Verona. In: PMLA., vol. 48, 1933, pp. 767–76.

KING HENRY VI (Parts I–III)

(page 196)

(1) LITERARY GENESIS

The Whole Contention (1619). Printed in: The Shakespeare quarto facsimiles. London, 1886.

THOMAS KENNY: King Henry VI, Parts I–III. In his The life and genius of Shakespeare. London, 1864, pp. 245–367.
Devotes a large portion of his book to H. VI.

J. M. ROBERTSON: Mr. Shaw and 'The Maid'. London, 1926. (vi, 115 pp.)
Rev.: TLS. Jan. 21, 1926, p. 46.
Denies Shakespeare any participation in 1 H. VI and attributes it to Marlowe, Green, and Peele.

MADELEINE DORAN: Henry VI, Parts II and III, their relation to the Contention and the True Tragedy. Univ. of Iowa, 1928. (88 pp.)=Univ. of Iowa Humanistic Studies, vol. 4, no. 4.

B. A. P. VAN DAM: Shakespeare problems nearing solution. Henry VI and Richard III. In: Engl. Studies, vol. 12, 1930, pp. 81–97.

J. M. ROBERTSON: The 2nd and 3rd parts of Henry VI. In his The Shakespeare canon. Part 4, Division II. London, 1932. (183 pp.)

R. B. MCKERROW: A note on Henry VI, part II, and the Contention of York and Lancaster. In: RESt., vol. 9, 1933, pp. 157–69.

CLAYTON ALVIS GREER: The York and Lancaster quarto-folio sequence. In: PMLA., vol. 48, 1933, pp. 655–704.
Supports, in opposition to Peter Alexander and Madeleine Doran, Tucker Brooke's opinion (1912). Cf. PMLA., vol. 50, 1935, pp. 919–20 (W. W. Greg).

MARION A. TAYLOR: Lord Cobham and Shakespeare's Duchess of Gloucester. In: The Sh. Assoc. Bull., vol. 9, 1934, pp. 150–6.

LUCILLE KING: The use of Hall's chronicles in the Folio and Quarto texts of Henry VI. In: Phil. Quart., vol. 13, 1934, pp. 321–32.

LUCILLE KING: 2 and 3 Henry VI—which Holinshed? In: PMLA., vol. 50, 1935, pp. 745–52.
Proves that Shakespeare used the 1587 Holinshed and not the first edition.

KING RICHARD III

(*page* 198)

(1) THE TEXT

The Bankside Shakespeare. Vol. 15: King Richard III [parallel impression of Q 1597 and F]. Ed. by ELIAS A. CALKINS. New York, 1891. (lvii, 239 pp.)

ROBERT W. BABCOCK: An introduction to the study of the text of 'Richard III'. In: Stud. in Phil., vol. 24, 1927, pp. 243–60.

JAMES RUSSELL LOWELL: Shakespeare's Richard III. In his Latest literary essays and addresses. London, 1891, pp. 111–30.

B. A. P. VAN DAM: Shakespeare problems nearing a solution. Henry VI and Richard III. In: Engl. Studies, vol. 12, 1930, pp. 81–97.

CLAYTON A. GREER: The relation of Richard III to the True Tragedy of Richard Duke of York and the Third Part of Henry VI. In: Stud. in Phil., vol. 29, 1932, pp. 543–50.

EDLEEN BEGG: Shakespeare's debt to Hall and Holinshed in Richard III. In: Stud. in Phil., vol. 32, 1935, pp. 189–96.

(3) DRAMATIC ART

(b) *Art of Characterization*

KARL SCHMIDT: Margareta von Anjou vor und bei Shakespeare. Diss. Berlin, 1905. (29 S.) Enlarged in: Palaestra, 54. Berlin, 1906. (xi, 286 S.) Rev.: Sh. Jb. 44, 1908, S. 336–7, Churchill; Bbl. 20, 1909, S. 244–5, Konr. Meier.

A. LESCHTSCH: Richard III. Eine Charakterstudie. Berlin, 1908. (34 S.)= Neue Shakespeare-Bühne, hrsg. v. Erich Paetel, 5. Rev.: Sh. Jb. 45, 1909, S. 337–8, George B. Churchill; Arch. 122, 1909, S. 214–15, A. Brandl.

JUTTA HOLTZ: Abnorme Charaktere bei Shakespeare: Othello, Richard III., Macbeth. Diss. Tübingen, 1933. (47 S.)

(3*) MISCELLANEOUS TREATISES

JOHN WEBSTER SPARGO: Clarence in the malmsey-butt. In: MLN., vol. 51, 1936, pp. 166–73.

KING RICHARD II

(*page* 201)

(1) THE TEXT

The Bankside Shakespeare. Vol. 17: King Richard II [parallel impression of Q 1597 and F]. Ed. by ALFRED WAITES. New York, 1892. (xlv, 173 pp.)

(2) LITERARY GENESIS

L. RIECHELMANN: Zu Richard II. Shakespeare und Holinshed. Progr. Plauen, 1860. (26 S.)

FREDERICK S. BOAS: A pre-Shakespearean Richard II. In: Fortn. Rev., vol. 122, 1902, pp. 391–404.

(3) MISCELLANEOUS TREATISES ON RICHARD II

RAY HEFFNER: Shakespeare, Hayward, and Essex. In: PMLA., vol. 45, 1930, pp. 754–80.

EVELYN MAY ALBRIGHT: Shakespeare's Richard II, Hayward's History of Henry IV, and the Essex conspiracy. In: PMLA., vol. 46, 1931, pp. 694–719. Cp. also: PMLA., vol. 47, 1932, pp. 898–901.

ROMEO AND JULIET
(*page* 202)
(1) THE TEXT

The Bankside Shakespeare. Vol. 5: Romeo and Juliet [parallel impression of Q 1597 and F]. Ed. by B. RUSH FIELD. New York, 1889. (209 pp.)

F. G. FLEAY: The text of Romeo and Juliet. In: Macm. Mag. 1877, no. 213.

(2) LITERARY GENESIS

Brooke's Romeus and Juliet and Painter's Rhomeo and Julietta, ed. by P. A. DANIEL. In: Trans. New Sh. Soc. 1875. Ser. III, part I. (xl, 144 pp.)

W. KLINGBEIL: Der poetische Wert der beiden ersten Quartos von Shakespeares 'Romeo and Juliet' und die Art ihrer Entstehung. Diss. Königsberg, 1907. (127 S.)

MAX J. WOLFF: Ein Beitrag zur Geschichte des Stoffes von 'Romeo und Julia'. In: Zs. f. vgl. Lit. gesch., N.F., Bd. 17, 1909, S. 439–41.

JOHN ERSKINE: 'Romeo and Juliet'. In: Shakespearian Studies, ed. by B. MATTHEWS and A. H. THORNDIKE. New York, 1916, pp. 215–34.

OLIN H. MOORE: The origins of the legend of Romeo and Juliet in Italy. In: Speculum, vol. 5, 1930, pp. 264–77.

VITTORIO BETTELONI: La storia di Giulietta e Romeo. Con una 'Avertenza' sul Museo Shakespeariano di Gianfranco Betteloni. Verona, 1934. (82 pp.)

A. TRAMPE BÖDTKER: Arthur Brooke and his poem. In: E. St., Bd. 70, 1935, S. 167–8.

(5) SUBSEQUENT HISTORY OF THE PLAY
(a) Adaptations and Translations

Die erste deutsche Romeo-Übersetzung [von SYMON GRYNÄUS, 1758], hrsg. von ERNST HEINRICH MENSEL. Northampton, Mass. 1933. (xxvi, 88 pp.)= Smith College Stud. in mod. lang., vol. 14, nos. 3–4. Rev.: Bbl. 45, 1934, S. 109–12, Elise Deckner; Sh. Jb. 70, 1934, S. 148–9, Hans Hecht. New impression of 'Neue Probestücke der englischen Schaubühne', Basel, 1758, with careful introduction.

HANS KÜRY: Simon Grynaeus von Basel (1725–1799), der erste deutsche Übersetzer von Shakespeares Romeo and Julia. Zürich, 1935. (83 S.)= Basler Beiträge z. dt. Literatur- u. Geistesgesch. Bd. 2.

A MIDSUMMER NIGHT'S DREAM

(page 206)

(1) THE TEXT

The Bankside Shakespeare. Vol. 8: A Midsummer Night's Dream [parallel impression of Q 1600 and F]. Ed. by WILLIAM REYNOLDS. New York, 1890. (159 pp.)

(2) LITERARY GENESIS

JAMES O. HALLIWELL: Illustrations of the fairy mythology of a 'Midsummer Night's Dream'. London, Sh. Soc., 1845. (xxii, 320 pp.)

WILLIAM BELL: Shakespeare's Puck and his folklore, illustrated from the superstitions of a ℐnations. London, 1852.

E. K. CHAMBERS: The occasion of 'A Midsummer Night's Dream'. In: A book of homage to Shakespeare, ed. by ISRAEL GOLLANCZ. London, 1916, pp. 154–60.

MARGARET L. FARRAND: An additional source for 'A Midsummer Night's Dream'. In: Stud. in Phil., vol. 27, 1930, pp. 233–43.

A. G. VAN KRANENDONK: Spenserian echoes in A Midsummer-Night's Dream. In: Engl. Studies, vol. 14, 1932, pp. 209–17.

WOLFGANG KELLER: Die Entstehung des Sommernachtstraums. In: Anglia, Bd. 59, 1935, S. 376–84.

(2*) ART OF CHARACTERIZATION

JOHN BOYNTON PRIESTLEY: Bully Bottom. In his The English comic characters. London, 1925, pp. 1–19.

(3) SUBSEQUENT HISTORY OF THE PLAY

GEORGE C. D. ODELL: 'A Midsummer Night's Dream' on the New York stage. In: Shakespearian Studies, ed. by B. MATTHEWS and A. H. THORNDIKE. New York, 1916, pp. 119–62.

THE TAMING OF THE SHREW

(page 208)

Bibliography

TALCOTT WILLIAMS: A bibliography of 'The Taming of the Shrew'. I: Editions and related plays. In: Shakespeariana, vol. 5, Philadelphia, 1888, pp. 449–56.

(1) THE TEXT

The Bankside Shakespeare. Vol. 2: The Taming of the Shrew [parallel impression of 'The Taming of a Shrew' 1594 and F]. Ed. by ALBERT F. FREY. New York, 1888. (278 pp.)

(2) LITERARY GENESIS

H. B. CHARLTON: The Taming of the Shrew. In: Bull. John Rylands Libr., vol. 16, 1932, pp. 353–75.

(3) SUBSEQUENT HISTORY OF THE PLAY

Kunst über alle Künste, ein bös Weib gut zu machen. Eine deutsche Bearbeitung von Shakespeares The Taming of the Shrew aus dem Jahre 1672. Neu hrsg. von REINHOLD KÖHLER. Berlin, 1864. (xliii, 268 S.)

KING JOHN

(page 210)

(1) LITERARY GENESIS

The Bankside Shakespeare. Vol. 18: King John [parallel impression of 'The Troublesome Raigne' 1591 and F]. Ed. by APPLETON MORGAN. New York, 1892. (xx, 307 pp.)

G. B. HARRISON: Shakespeare's topical significances. I. King John. In: TLS. Nov. 13, 1930, p. 939.

THE MERCHANT OF VENICE

(page 211)

(1) THE TEXT

The Bankside Shakespeare. Vol. 3: The Merchant of Venice [parallel impression of Q 1600 and F]. Ed. by ERNEST WHITNEY. New York, 1888. (207 pp.)

(2) LITERARY GENESIS

SIDNEY LEE: The original of Shylock. In: Gentleman's Mag., Feb. 1880.

S. A. SMALL: 'The Jew'. In: MLR., vol. 26, 1931, pp. 281–7.

MARGARET SCHLAUCH: The pound of flesh story in the north. In: JEGPh., vol. 30, 1931, pp. 348–60.

J. L. CARDOZO: The background of Shakespeare's Merchant of Venice. In: Engl. Studies, vol. 14, 1932, pp. 177–86.

CECIL ROTH: The background of Shylock. In: RESt., vol. 9, 1933, pp. 148–56.

H. B. CHARLTON: Shakespeare's Jew. In: Bull. of the John Rylands Libr., vol. 18, 1934, pp. 34–68.

JOHN W. DRAPER: Usury in The Merchant of Venice. In: Mod. Phil., vol. 33, 1935, pp. 37–47.

(3) ART OF CHARACTERIZATION

ISRAEL GOLLANCZ: Bits of timber: some observations on Shakespearian names —'Shylock'; 'Polonius'; 'Malvolio'. In: A book of homage to Shakespeare, ed. by ISRAEL GOLLANCZ. London, 1916, pp. 170–8.

CELESTE T. WRIGHT: Some conventions regarding the usurer in Elizabethan literature. In: Stud. in Phil., vol. 31, 1934, pp. 176–97.

HAROLD R. WALLEY: Shakespeare's portrayal of Shylock. In: Parrott Presentation Volume, 1935, pp. 213–42.

(4) THE SHYLOCK PACT

RUDOLF VON IHERING: Der Kampf um's Recht. Wien, 1872. (100 S.)
Cf. in particular pp. 63–6.

MISS TOULMIN SMITH: On the bond-story in the Merchant of Venice, and a version of it in the Cursor Mundi. In: New Sh. Soc. Trans., 1875–6, pp. 181–9.

G. AZZOLINI: Shylock e la leggenda della libbra di carne. Reggio, 1893. (47 pp.)

(4*) *Miscellaneous treatises on the play*

P. A. DANIEL: A note on the Rev. N. J. Halpin's time-analysis of the Merchant of Venice. In: New Sh. Soc. Trans., 1877–9, pp. 41–57.

HARRIS J. GRISTON: Portia's Belmont located. In: The Sh. Assoc. Bull., vol. 7, 1932, pp. 162–73.

VIOLET M. JEFFERY: Shakespeare's Venice. In: MLR., vol. 27, 1932, pp. 24–35.

(5) SUBSEQUENT HISTORY OF THE PLAY

(a) *Adaptations*

FREDERICK T. WOOD: The Merchant of Venice in the 18th century. In: Engl. Studies, vol. 15, 1933, pp. 209–18.

(b) *The Merchant of Venice on the Stage*

J. HAROLD WILSON: Granville's 'stock-jobbing Jew'. In: Phil. Quart., vol. 13, 1934, pp. 1–15.

KING HENRY IV (Parts I and II)

(*page* 214)

(1) THE TEXT

The Bankside Shakespeare. Vols. 12, 13: King Henry IV [1st Part, parallel impression of Q 1598 and F; 2nd Part, parallel impression of Q 1600 and F]. Ed. by WILLIAM H. FLEMING. New York, 1890, 1891. (201 and 207 pp.)

(2) LITERARY GENESIS

R. P. COWL: Sources of the text of Henry IV. London, 1929. (54 pp.)

L. L. SCHÜCKING: The quarto of King Henry IV, part II. In: TLS. Sept. 25, 1930, p. 752.

ALFRED HART: Was the second part of King Henry the Fourth censored? In his Shakespeare and the homilies. O.U.P., 1934, pp. 154–218.

JOHN JAMES ELSON: The Non-Shakespearian Richard II and Shakespeare's Henry IV, part I. In: Stud. in Phil., vol. 32, 1935, pp. 177–88.

(3) DRAMATIC ART

GREGOR SARRAZIN: Falstaff, Pistol, Nym und ihre Urbilder=Kleine Shakespeare-Studien I. In: Beitr. z. roman. u. engl. Philol. Dem 10. Dt. Neuphilologentage überreicht. Breslau, 1902, S. 177–97.

L. W. V. HARCOURT: The two Sir John Fastolfs. In: Trans. Royal Histor. Soc., 3rd ser., vol. 4, 1910, pp. 47–62.

JOHN BOYNTON PRIESTLEY: Falstaff and his circle. In his The English comic characters. London, 1925, pp. 69–105.

S. ASA SMALL: The structure of Falstaff's humor. In: The Sh. Assoc. Bull., vol. 7, 1932, pp. 114–22.

JOHN W. DRAPER: Sir John Falstaff. In: RESt., vol. 8, 1932, pp. 414–24.

CUMBERLAND CLARK: Falstaff and his friends. Shrewsbury, 1935. (128 pp.)

H. B. CHARLTON: Falstaff. In: Bull. John Rylands Libr., vol. 19, 1935, pp. 46–89.

(4) MISCELLANEOUS TREATISES

HELEN E. SANDISON: The Ninth Earl of Northumberland quotes his ancestor Hotspur. In: RESt., vol. 12, 1936, pp. 71–5.

KING HENRY V
(page 216)
(1) THE TEXT

The Bankside Shakespeare. Vol. 16: King Henry V [parallel impression of Q 1600 and F]. Ed. by HENRY PAINE STOKES. New York, 1892. (263 pp.)

BARBARA DAMON SIMISON: Stage directions: A test for the playhouse origin of the First Quarto Henry V. In: Phil. Quart., vol. 11, 1932, pp. 39–56.

HEREWARD T. PRICE: The quarto and folio texts of Henry V. In: Phil. Quart., vol. 12, 1933, pp. 24–32.

GERDA OKERLUND: The quarto version of Henry V as a stage adaptation. In: PMLA., vol. 49, 1934, pp. 810–34.

(2) LITERARY GENESIS

EDWARD OWEN: Ludovic Lloyd, a long-forgotten Welshman, a contemporary and possible acquaintance of William Shakespeare, and the possible exemplar of Shakespeare's 'Fluellen'. Wrexham, 1931. (24 pp.)

M. L. RADOFF: Influence of the French farce in Henry V and the Merry Wives. In: MLN., vol. 48, 1933, pp. 427–35.

(3) DRAMATIC ART

ELMER EDGAR STOLL: Henry V. In his Poets and playwrights. Minneapolis, 1930, pp. 31–54.

R. G. MOULTON: On character development in Shakespeare as illustrated by Macbeth and King Henry V. In: Trans. New Sh. Soc., 1880–6, no. xxv.

THE MERRY WIVES OF WINDSOR
(page 217)
(1) THE TEXT

The Bankside Shakespeare. Vol. 1: The Merry Wives of Windsor [parallel impression of Q 1602 and F]. Ed. by APPLETON MORGAN. New York, 1888. (220 pp.)

(2) LITERARY GENESIS

HERMANN KURZ: Zu Shakespeare's Leben und Schaffen. Altes und Neues. München, 1868. (155 S.)
Cp. in particular chap. I: Von Mömpelgart nach Windsor. S. 7–58.

GREGOR SARRAZIN: Falstaff, Pistol, Nym und ihre Urbilder. In his Kleine Sh. Studien. Breslau, 1902.

GREGOR SARRAZIN: Nym und Ben Jonson. In: Sh. Jb., Jg. 40, 1904, S. 213–22.

CARL WINCKLER: Marston's Erstlingswerke und ihre Beziehungen zu Shakespeare. In: E. St., Bd. 33, 1904, S. 216–24.

WILLIAM VOLLHARDT: Ein italienischer Falstaff. In: Stud. z. vgl. Lit. gesch., Bd. 7, 1907, S. 110–17.
Treats of the possibility of a connexion between Shakespeare's play and the Italian comedy 'Atalanta' (Udine, 1610).

JOSEPH DE PEROTT: Falstaff und der Dreieinigkeitsbruder bei Feliciano de Silva. In: GRM., Bd. 2, 1910, S. 633–4.

LESLIE HOTSON: Shakespeare versus Shallow. London, 1931. (376 pp.) Rev.: TLS. Oct. 1, 1931, p. 749; Life and Letters, 7, 1931, pp. 356–62, Augustine Birrell; The Sh. Assoc. Bull. 6, 1931, pp. 183–4, Sam. A. Tannenbaum; Rev. anglo-amér. 9, 1932, pp. 224–32, F. C. Danchin; MLR. 27, 1932, pp. 218–21, W. W. Greg; Arch. 161, 1932, S. 115–16, A. Brandl; MLN. 47, 1932, pp. 399–402, Felix E. Schelling; The Sh. Assoc. Bull, 7, 1932, pp. 174–82, John E. Hannigan.

OSCAR JAMES CAMPBELL: The Italianate background of 'The Merry Wives of Windsor'. In: Essays and Studies in Engl. and comparative literature. Univ. of Michigan Pr., 1932, pp. 81–117.

M. L. RADOFF: Influence of the French farce in Henry V and The Merry Wives. In: MLN., vol. 48, 1933, pp. 427–35.

JULIUS CAESAR
(*page* 218)
(2) LITERARY GENESIS

F. G. FLEAY: On two plays of Shakespeare's, the versions of which as we have them are the results of alterations by other hands. II. Julius Caesar. In: New Sh. Soc. Trans., ser. 1, no. 1, 1874, pp. 357–66.

PERCY SIMPSON: The date of Shakespeare's Julius Caesar. In: N. & Q., 9th ser., vol. 3, 1899, pp. 105 and 216.

ALGERNON DE VIVIER TASSIN: Julius Caesar. In: Shakespearian Studies, ed. by B. MATTHEWS and A. H. THORNDIKE. New York, 1916, pp. 255–87.

MARTIN ELLEHAUGE: The use of his sources made by Shakespeare in Julius Caesar and Antony and Cleopatra. In: E. St., Bd. 65, 1930/1, S. 197–210.

INGEBORG ALTKAMP: Die Gestaltung Caesars bei Plutarch und Shakespeare. Diss. Bonn, 1933. (vi, 70 S.)

LORENZ MORSBACH: Shakespeares Caesarbild. Halle, 1935. 32 S.=Stud. z. engl. Phil., H. 88.

(3) DRAMATIC ART

FRIEDRICH GUNDOLF: Caesar und Brutus. In: Europ. Revue, Jg. 4, 1928, S. 489–513.

G. WILSON KNIGHT: Brutus. An essay in poetic interpretation. In: Church Quart. Rev., vol. 110, 1930, pp. 40–71.

(4) EXPLANATORY WORKS

H. GAUDIG: Julius Caesar. In his Wegweiser durch die klassischen Schuldramen. 4. Abt. Leipzig, 1899, ²1905, S. 355–409.

(6) SUBSEQUENT HISTORY OF THE PLAY

WALTER PAETOW: Die erste metrische deutsche Shakespeare-Übersetzung in ihrer Stellung zu ihrer Literaturepoche. Diss. Bern, 1893. (82 S.)
Deals with Borcke's translation of Julius Caesar.

FRIEDRICH GUNDELFINGER (GUNDOLF): Caesar in der deutschen Literatur. Berlin, 1904. (vi, 129 S.)=Palaestra, 33.

RICHARD MARIA WERNER: Hebbels Theaterbearbeitung von Shakespeares 'Julius Caesar'. Nach ungedrucktem Material mitgeteilt. In: Zs. f. d. österr. Gymnasien, Jg. 58, 1907, S. 385–99.

MUCH ADO ABOUT NOTHING
(page 221)
(1) THE TEXT

The Bankside Shakespeare. Vol. 6: Much adoe about nothing [parallel impression of Q 1600 and F]. Ed. by WILLIAM H. FLEMING. New York, 1889. (209 pp.)

(2) LITERARY GENESIS

JULIA GRACE WALES: Shakespeare's use of English and foreign elements in the setting of 'Much Ado about Nothing'. In: Trans. Wisconsin Acad. of Science, Arts and Letters, vol. 28, 1933, pp. 363–98.

ALLISON GAW: Is Shakespeare's Much Ado a revised earlier play? In: PMLA., vol. 50, 1935, pp. 715–38.

(3) MISCELLANEOUS TREATISES ON THE PLAY

Much ado about nothing. Parallel passage edition, ed. by ALPHONSO GERALD NEWCOMER, completed by HENRY DAVID GRAY. Stanford Univ. Pr., 1929. (275 pp.)=Stanford Univ. Publ., Language and Literature, vol. 1, no. 2. Rev.: JEGPh. 30, 1931, pp. 590–2, H. T. Price.

NADINE PAGE: The public repudiation of Hero. In: PMLA., vol. 50, 1935, pp. 739–44.

NADINE PAGE: Beatrice: 'My Lady Disdain'. In: MLN., vol. 50, 1935, pp. 494–9.

(4) SUBSEQUENT HISTORY OF THE PLAY

JOHANNES BOLTE: Deutsche Verwandte von Shakespeares 'Viel Lärm um Nichts'. In: Sh. Jb., Jg. 21, 1886, S. 310–12.

AS YOU LIKE IT

(*page* 222)

(1) LITERARY GENESIS

HERMANN CONRAD: Die Erzählung von Gamelyn als Quelle zu Shakespeares 'As you like it'. In: Sh. Jb., Jg. 46, 1910, S. 120–2.

EDNA DAVIS ROMIG: 'As you like it'. Shakespeare's use of his source, Lodge's 'Rosalynde'. In: Univ. of Colorado Studies, vol. 16, 1929, pp. 300–22.

EDGAR I. FRIPP: 'Monsieur Jaques', 'Mounsir What-Ye-Call't'. In his Shakespeare Studies. O.U.P., 1930, pp. 151–68.

HERMAN COHEN: The Seven Ages of man. In: TLS. Jan. 30, 1930. p. 78.

CUMBERLAND CLARK: A study of 'As you like it'. London, 1932. (vi, 118 pp.)

MAX DEUTSCHBEIN: Shakespeares Kritik an Montaigne in 'As you like it'. In: Neuphilol. Monatsschr., Jg. 5, 1934, S. 369–85.

(1*) ART OF CHARACTERIZATION

JOHN BOYNTON PRIESTLEY: Touchstone. In his The English comic characters. London, 1925, pp. 20–42.

Z. S. FINK: Jaques and the Malcontent traveler. In: Phil. Quart., vol. 14, 1935, pp. 237–52.

OSCAR J. CAMPBELL: Jaques. In: Huntington Libr. Bull., no. 8, 1935, pp. 71–102.

MISCELLANEOUS TREATISES

R. G. MOULTON: On the humour of 'Love's Labour 's Lost' and 'As you like it'. In: Trans. New Sh. Soc., 1887–92, no. xii.

P. V. KREIDER: Genial literary satire in the Forest of Arden. In: The Sh. Assoc. Bull., vol. 10, 1935, pp. 212–31.

TWELFTH NIGHT

(*page* 223)

(1) THE TEXT

SAMUEL A. TANNENBAUM: Comments on Twelfth Night. In his Shaksperian scraps and other Elizabethan fragments. New York, 1933, pp. 118–28.

(2) LITERARY GENESIS

JOSEPH DE PEROTT: Noch eine eventuelle Quelle zum Heiligen Dreikönigs-abend. In: Sh. Jb., Jg. 46, 1910, S. 118–20.

ALWIN THALER: The original Malvolio? In: The Sh. Assoc. Bull., vol. 7, 1932, pp. 57–71.
Proposes as model for Malvolio William Ffarington, Esquire (1537–1610), of Worden, Lancashire, steward (until 1594) to Lord Ferdinando Strange, Earl of Derby and patron of Shakespeare's company.

PAUL MUESCHKE and JEANNETTE FLEISHER: Jonsonian elements in the comic underplot of Twelfth Night. In: PMLA., vol. 48, 1933, pp. 722–40.

JOHN W. DRAPER: Olivia's household. In: PMLA., vol. 49, 1934, pp. 797–806.

(3) MISCELLANEOUS TREATISES

A. C. BRADLEY: Feste the jester. In: A book of homage to Shakespeare, ed. by ISRAEL GOLLANCZ. London, 1916, pp. 164–9.

ISRAEL GOLLANCZ: Some observations on Shakespearian names—'Shylock'; 'Polonius'; 'Malvolio'. In: A book of homage to Shakespeare, ed. by ISRAEL GOLLANCZ. London, 1916, pp. 170–8.

JOHN BOYNTON PRIESTLEY: The Illyrians. In his The English comic characters. London, 1925, pp. 43–68.
Characterization of Sir Toby Belch and Sir Andrew Aguecheek.

LOUIS B. WRIGHT: A conduct book for Malvolio. In: Stud. in Phil., vol. 31, 1934, pp. 115–32.
Refers to Darell's short discourse of the life of serving men, 1578.

HAMLET

(page 224)

(1) THE TEXT

(a) *Oldest Prints in Reprints*

Hamlet. The second quarto, 1604. A facsimile . . . by WILLIAM GRIGGS. Cf. THOMAS MARC PARROTT: Errors and omissions in the Griggs facsimile of the 2nd quarto of Hamlet. In: MLN., vol. 49, 1934, pp. 376–9.

The Bankside Shakespeare. Vol. 11: Hamlet [parallel impression of Q 1603 and F]. Ed. by EDWARD P. VINING. New York, 1890. (cli, 255 pp.)

Shakespeare's Hamlet. The first quarto 1603, reprod. in facsimile from the copy in the Henry E. Huntington Library. Cambridge, Mass., Harv. Univ. Pr., 1931. (6+64 pp.) Rev.: Bbl. 43, 1932, S. 127, H. Jantzen; Lbl. 53, 1932, Sp. 316/17, W. Fischer; RESt. 8, 1932, 369–70, R. B. McKerrow.

(b) *Later Editions*

HENRY N. PAUL: Players' quartos and duodecimos of Hamlet. In: MLN., vol. 49, 1934, pp. 369–75.

(c) *Treatises on the History of the Text*

C. H. HERFORD and W. H. WIDGERY: The first quarto edition of Hamlet, 1603. Two essays. London, 1880. (204 pp.) Rev.: E. St. 4, 1881, pp. 341–3, O. S. Seemann; Anglia, 4, 1881, Anzeiger, S. 27–44, G. Tanger.

B. A. P. VAN DAM: Are there interpolations in the text of Hamlet? In: A book of homage to Shakespeare, ed. by ISRAEL GOLLANCZ. London, 1916, pp. 473–80.

GERTRUDE SOUTHWICK KINGSLAND: The first quarto of Hamlet in the light of the stage. Oshkosh, Wis., 1923. (vi, 63 pp.)

GIOVANNI RAMELLO: Studi sugli apocrifi Shakespeariani. The tragicall historie of Hamlet, Prince of Denmarke, 1603. Con un' appendice sul testo anonimo Der bestrafte Brudermord oder Prinz Hamlet aus Dänemark. Torino, 1930. (vii, 293 pp.) Rev.: TLS. June 12, 1930, p. 492; RESt. 7, 1931, pp. 97–100, W. W. Greg; Dt. Litztg., 3. Folge, Jg. 1, 1930, Sp. 1175–7, M. J. Wolff; MLN. 46, 1931, pp. 410–12, H. D. Gray; Bbl. 42, 1931, S. 120–1, H. Jantzen.

LEVIN L. SCHÜCKING: Zum Problem der Überlieferung des Hamlet-Textes. Leipzig, 1931. (42 S.)=Verhandl. Sächs. Akad. d. Wiss., Phil.-hist. Kl., Bd. 83, 1931, Heft 4. Rev.: RESt. 8, 1932, pp. 228–31, W. W. Greg; Engl. Studies, 14, 1932, pp. 88–90, B. A. P. van Dam; Lbl. 54, 1933, Sp. 19–20, Helene Richter.

HENRY DAVID GRAY: The date of Hamlet. In: JEGPh., vol. 31, 1932, pp. 51–61.

JOHN DOVER WILSON: The manuscript of Shakespeare's Hamlet and the problems of its transmission. 2 vols. C.U.P., 1934. (xvii, 435 pp.)=Shakespeare Problems, by A. W. POLLARD and J. DOVER WILSON. Vol. 4. Rev.: TLS. 1934, p. 563; MLR. 30, 1935, pp. 80–6, W. W. Greg; Bbl. 46, 1935, S. 97–104, 129–37, L. L. Schücking.

ALFRED HART: The vocabulary of the first quarto of Hamlet. In: RESt., vol. 12, 1936, pp. 18–30.

(2) LITERARY GENESIS

(b) *Sources and related material*

R. G. LATHAM: Two dissertations on the Hamlet of Saxo Grammaticus and of Shakespeare. I. The historical personality of Hamlet. II. The relation of the Hamlet of Shakespeare to the German play Prinz Hamlet aus Dänemark. London, 1872. (150 pp.)

ANDREAS HEUSLER: Amlethus. In: Reallexikon d. germ. Altertumskunde, hrsg. v. JOH. HOOPS. Bd. 1, Strassburg, 1911–13, S. 78–9.

CORPUS HAMLETICUM. Hamlet in Sage und Dichtung, Kunst und Musik. Hsrg. von JOSEF SCHICK. Bd. 2. Das Glückskind mit dem Todesbrief. Europäische Sagen des Mittelalters und ihr Verhältnis zum Orient. Leipzig, 1932. (x, 405 S.) Bd. 4. Die Scharfsinnsproben. 1. Teil: Der fernere Orient. Leipzig, 1934. (xii, 450 S.) Rev.: MLR., vol. 30, 1935, pp. 520–1, G. C. Moore Smith; Sh. Jb. 71, 1935, S. 117–18, W. Keller.

HERMANN SCHNEIDER: Amled. In his Germanische Heldensage. Bd. 2, Abt. I, Buch II. Berlin, 1933, S. 225–50.

(c) *The Ur-Hamlet*

GREGOR SARRAZIN: Die Entstehung der Hamlet-Tragödie. I. Shakespeare's Hamlet und Thomas Kyd. In: Anglia, Bd. 12, 1889, S. 143–57.

M. W. MACCALLUM: The authorship of the early Hamlet. In: An English miscellany presented to Dr. Furnivall in honour of his 75th birthday. Oxford, 1901, pp. 282–95.

JOHN W. CUNLIFFE: Nash and the earlier Hamlet. In: PMLA., vol. 21, N.S., vol. 14, 1906, pp. 193–9.

(d) *The 'Bestrafte Brudermord'*

A. PINLOCHE: De Shakespearii Hamleto et germanica tragoedia quae inscribitur: Der bestrafte Brudermord, oder Prinz Hamlet aus Dänemark, quantopere inter se distent aut congruant. Paris, 1890. (51 pp.)

(e) *Further Literary Relations*

SUSANNE TÜRCK: Shakespeare und Montaigne. Ein Beitrag zur Hamlet-Frage. Berlin, 1930. (v, 160 S.)=Neue Forschung. H. 8. Rev.: Bbl. 42, 1931, S. 124–6, H. Jantzen; Lbl. 54, 1933, Sp. 17–19, E. A. Philippson; Neophilologus, 19, 1934, pp. 128–9, H. de Groot.

HAROLD R. WALLEY: The dates of Hamlet and Marston's The Malcontent. In: RESt., vol. 9, 1933, pp. 397–409.
'There is every reason to place Hamlet before the registry date of July 1602, and not a scrap of evidence to show that the Malcontent could antedate 1604.'

PERCY SIMPSON: The theme of revenge in Elizabethan tragedy. O.U.P., 1935. (28 pp.)=Annual Sh. lecture of the Brit. Acad. 1935=Proc. Brit. Acad., vol. 21.

(3) DRAMATIC ART

(a) *General Essays*

L. L. SCHÜCKING: The churchyard-scene in Shakespeare's Hamlet, v. 1, an after-thought? In: RESt., vol. 11, 1935, pp. 129–38.

JOHN DOVER WILSON: What happens in Hamlet. C.U.P., 1935. (viii, 335 pp.) Rev.: TLS. Oct. 10, 1935, 617–18 (leading article); MLR. 31, 1936, pp. 145–54, W. W. Greg.

(b) *Art of Characterization*

ISRAEL GOLLANCZ: Some observations on Shakespearian names—'Shylock'; 'Polonius'; 'Malvolio'. In: A book of homage to Shakespeare, ed. by ISRAEL GOLLANCZ. London, 1916, pp. 170–8.

BERNHARD SCHERER: Polonius, der Typus des Senilen. Eine psychiatrische Shakespeare-Studie. In: Anglia, Bd. 54, 1930, S. 149–67.

JOHN W. DRAPER: The elder Hamlet and the ghost. In: The Sh. Assoc. Bull., vol. 9, 1934, pp. 75–82.

JOHN W. DRAPER: Queen Gertrude. In: Revue anglo-amér., vol. 12, 1934, pp. 20–34.

JOHN W. DRAPER: Hamlet's schoolfellows. In: E. St., Bd. 69, 1934/5, S. 350–66.

JOHN W. DRAPER: Ophelia and Laertes. In: Phil. Quart., vol. 14, 1935, pp. 38–53.

JOHN W. DRAPER: Shakespeare's italianate courtier, Osric. In: Rev. de litt. comp., vol. 15, 1935, pp. 289–97.

E. K. BROADUS: Polonius. In: Univ. of Toronto Quart., vol. 4, 1935, no. 3, pp. 337–55.

JOHN W. DRAPER: Lord Chamberlain Polonius. In: Sh. Jb., Bd. 71, 1935, S. 78–93.

J. P. MALLESON: Was King Claudius a usurper? In: TLS. Jan. 4, 1936, p. 15.

(5) AESTHETIC CRITICISM OF THE PLAY AND ANALYSIS OF THE CHARACTER
OF THE HERO

CHRISTIAN GARVE: Über die Rollen der Wahnwitzigen in Shakespeares Schauspielen, und über den Charakter Hamlets insbesondere. In: Versuche über verschiedene Gegenstände aus der Moral, der Literatur und dem gesellschaftlichen Leben. 2. Teil. Breslau, 1796, S. 431–510.

JOHN CONOLLY: A study of 'Hamlet'. London, 1863. (210 pp.)

HENRY BLAZE DE BURY: 'Hamlet' et ses commentateurs depuis Goethe. In: RDM., vol. 74, 1868, pp. 409–47.

ROCCO DE ZERBI: Amleto, studio psicologico. Torino, 1880. (80 pp.)

BERNHARD TEN BRINK in: Shakespeare. 5 Vorlesungen aus dem Nachlass. Strassburg, 1893.

CHRISTOPH VON SCHRÖDER: Wille und Nervosität in Shakespeare's Hamlet. Ein Versuch, Hamlets Naturell vom medizinischen Standpunkte zu beleuchten. Riga, 1893. (ii, 37 S.)

ANTON DELBRÜCK: Über Hamlets Wahnsinn. Vortrag. Hamburg, 1893=Slg. gemeinverständl. wiss. Vorträge, N.F., 8. Serie, No. 172.

S. LANDMANN: Zur Diagnose psychischer Vorgänge, mit besonderer Bezugnahme auf Hamlets Geisteszustand. In: Zs. f. Psychologie u. Physiologie d. Sinne, Bd. 11, 1896.

ELMER EDGAR STOLL: Shakespeare, Marston, and the Malcontent type. In: Mod. Phil., vol. 3, 1906, pp. 281–303.

A. J. A. WALDOCK: Hamlet. A study in critical method. C.U.P., 1931. (99 pp.)
Rev.: TLS. Oct. 8, 1931, p. 772; MLR. 27, 1932, pp. 84–5, Peter Alexander; Engl. Studies, 14, 1932, pp. 166–8, H. de Groot; RESt. 9, 1933, pp. 332–5, P. L. Carver.
Gives a summary of the history of ideas about Hamlet.

IRVING T. RICHARDS: The meaning of Hamlet's soliloquy. In: PMLA., vol. 48, 1933, pp. 741–66.

HAROLD R. WALLEY: Shakespeare's conception of Hamlet. In: PMLA., vol. 48, 1933, pp. 777–98.

M. YEARSLEY: The sanity of Hamlet. London, 1933. (vii, 101 pp.)

OTTO HINRICHSEN: Der verständliche—unverstandene Hamlet. In: Schweizer Arch. f. Neurologie u. Psychiatrie, Bd. 31/32, Zürich, 1933. (33 S.)

ANNELIESE THOMAS: Don Carlos und Hamlet. Bonn, 1933. (120 S.)=Mnemosyne. Heft 15.
Confrontation of these two dramatic personalities.

ERNST WEIGELIN: Hamlet-Studien. Beiträge zur Hamletkritik. Stuttgart, 1934. (viii, 113 S.) Rev.: Zs. f. frz. u. engl. Unterr. 33, 1934, S. 349–50, Wolfg. Keller; Sh. Jb. 71, 1935, S. 118–20, Wolfg. Keller.

HEINZ NICOLAI: 'Ecstasy' und 'passion'. Ein Beitrag zur Deutung des Hamletcharakters. In: GRM., Jg. 23, 1935, S. 37–67.

IWAN TURGENEW: Hamlet und Don Quixote.=Einleitung zu Miguel de Cervantes: Don Quixote. 2 Bde. Leipzig, 1935.

E. WEIGELIN: Hamlets Verschickung nach England. Ein Beitrag zur Hamletkritik. In: Arch., Jg. 90, Bd. 167, 1935, S. 193–200.

ELMER EDGAR STOLL: Hamlet the man. London, 1935. (29 pp.)=The Engl. Assoc., Pamphl. 91.

LEVIN L. SCHÜCKING: Der Sinn des Hamlet. Kunstwerk, Handlung, Überlieferung. Leipzig, 1935. (132 S.) Rev.: Sh. Jb. 71, 1935, S. 116–17, W. Keller; JEGPh. 35, 1936, pp. 149–50, Tucker Brooke; Bbl. 47, 1936, S. 103–5, Walter Fischer.

HEINRICH CHRISTOPH MATTHES: 'Thus conscience does make cowards of us all' (Hamlet III, 1). In: Anglia, Bd. 60, 1936, S. 181–96.

HEINRICH MEYER-BENFEY: Das Problem des Hamlet. In: GRM., Jg. 24, 1936, S. 35–45.

Appendix: *The Play within the play*

W. T. MALLESON and J. R. SEELEY: Which are Hamlet's 'Dozen or sixteen lines'? In: New Sh. Soc. Trans., ser. 1, no. 2, 1874, pp. 465–98.

HANS SCHWAB: Das Schauspiel im Schauspiel zur Zeit Shaksperes. Wien & Leipzig, 1896. (viii, 97 S.)=Wiener Beitr. z. engl. Phil., Bd. 5. Rev: Bbl. 8, 1898, S. 65–71, Rud. Fischer.

W. W. GREG: A critical mouse trap. In: A book of homage to Shakespeare, ed. by ISRAEL GOLLANCZ. London, 1916, pp. 179–80.

RALPH DE SOMERI CHILDS: Influence of the court tragedy on the play scene in Hamlet. In: JEGPh., vol. 32, 1933, pp. 44–50.

G. BULLOUGH: 'The murder of Gonzago'. A probable source for Hamlet. In: MLR., vol. 30, 1935, pp. 433–44.

E. H. OLIPHANT: Hamlet's dozen lines. In: TLS. Aug. 29, 1935, p. 537. Cf. also: Sept. 5, 1935, p. 552, and Sept. 19, p. 565.

(7) HAMLET'S AGE AND NAME

(a) *Hamlet's Age*

E. SULLIVAN: Hamlet's age. In: Trans. New Sh. Soc., 1880–6, no. xxvii.

(b) *Hamlet's Name*

KEMP MALONE: On the etymology of Hamlet. In: Phil. Quart., vol. 4, 1925, pp. 158–60.

(8) SUBSEQUENT HISTORY OF THE PLAY

Stage Adaptations and productions

WILHELM WIDMANN: Hamlets Bühnenlaufbahn (1601–1877). Aus dem Nachlass hrsg. von JOSEPH SCHICK und WERNER DEETJEN. Leipzig, 1931. (xii, 276 S. u. Abb.)=Schriften d. Dt. Shakespeare-Ges., N.F. Bd. 1. Rev.: E. St. 66, 1932, S. 423–4, Albert Eichler; Litbl. 54, 1933, Sp. 107–8, Helene Richter; Engl. Studies, 15, 1933, pp. 193–7, H. de Groot.

NATALIE RICE CLARK: Hamlet on the Dial Stage. Paris, 1931. (471 pp.)

WALTER A. REICHART: A modern German Hamlet [The revision by Gerhart Hauptmann]. In: JEGPh., vol. 31, 1932, pp. 27–50.

GEORGE WINCHESTER STONE, JR.: Garrick's long lost alteration of Hamlet. In: PMLA., vol. 49, 1934, pp. 890–921.

HAROLD CHILD: The stage-history of Hamlet. In: The works of Shakespeare, ed. by JOHN DOVER WILSON [The New Cambr. Sh.]. Hamlet. 1934. pp. lxix–xcvii.

TROILUS AND CRESSIDA

(page 239)

(1) THE TEXT

The Bankside Shakespeare. Vol. 4: Troilus and Cressida [parallel impression of Q 1609 and F]. Ed. by APPLETON MORGAN. New York, 1889. (239 pp.)

SAMUEL A. TANNENBAUM: A critique of the text of 'Troilus and Cressida' I, II. In: The Sh. Assoc. Bull., vol. 9, 1934, pp. 55–74, 125–44.

SAMUEL A. TANNENBAUM: The Folio text of 'Troilus and Cressida'. In: The Sh. Assoc. Bull., vol. 9, 1934, pp. 198–214.

(2) LITERARY GENESIS

NATHANIEL E. GRIFFIN: Un-Homeric elements in the medieval story of Troy. In: JEGPh., vol. 7, 1908, pp. 32–52.

WOLFGANG KELLER: Shakespeares 'Troilus and Cressida'. In: Sh. Jb., Jg. 66, 1930, S. 182–207.

ELIZABETH STEIN: Caxton's Recuyell and Shakespeare's Troilus. In: MLN., vol. 45, 1930, pp. 144–6.

VINCENZO SAPIENZA: Shakespeare contro Omero. Milano, 1931. (151 pp.)

The story of Troilus, as told by B. de Saint-Maure, G. Boccaccio, G. Chaucer, and R. Henryson. With an introd. by R. K. GORDON. London, 1934. (xviii, 384 pp.)

W. B. DRAYTON HENDERSON: Shakespeare's Troilus and Cressida yet deeper in its tradition. In: Parrott Presentation Volume, 1935, pp. 127–56.

(3) MISCELLANEOUS LITERATURE

GEORGE C. TAYLOR: Shakespeare's attitude towards love and honor in Troilus and Cressida. In: PMLA., vol. 45, 1930, pp. 781–6.

G. WILSON KNIGHT: The metaphysics of 'Troilus and Cressida'. In: Dublin Review, 185, 1930, pp. 228–42.

(4) SUBSEQUENT HISTORY OF THE PLAY

JOHN S. P. TATLOCK: The Welsh 'Troilus and Cressida' and its relation to the Elizabethan drama. In: MLR., vol. 10, 1915, pp. 265–82.

MEASURE FOR MEASURE
(page 240)
(2) LITERARY GENESIS

ROBERT H. WILSON: The Mariana plot of Measure for Measure. In: Phil. Quart., vol. 9, 1930, pp. 341–50.

FREDERICK E. BUDD: Material for a study of the sources of Shakespeare's Measure for Measure. In: Rev. de litt. comp. 11, 1931, pp. 711–36.

(3) SHAKESPEARE'S ART IN MEASURE FOR MEASURE

HOXIE N. FAIRCHILD: The two Angelo's. In: The Sh. Assoc. Bull., vol. 6, 1931, pp. 53–9.

ALL'S WELL THAT ENDS WELL
(page 241)
(3) DRAMATIC ART

GEORGE PHILIP KRAPP: Parolles. In: Shakespearian Studies, ed. by B. MATTHEWS and A. H. THORNDIKE. New York, 1916, pp. 291–300.

KING LEAR
(page 242)
(1) THE TEXT

The Bankside Shakespeare. Vol. 10: King Lear [parallel impression of Q 1608 and F]. Ed. by A. A. ADEE. New York, 1890. (214 pp.)

MADELEINE DORAN: The text of King Lear. California, Stanford Univ. Pr., 1931. (148 pp.)=Stanford Univ. Publ. in lang. and lit., vol. 4, no. 2. Rev.: TLS. March 31, 1932, p. 227; JEGPh. 31, 1932, pp. 296–9, Robert M. Smith; E. St. 67, 1932, S. 272–4, Eduard Eckhardt; Rev. anglo-amér. 10, 1933, pp. 336–7, A. Koszul; MLR. 28, 1933, pp. 251–2, Geoffrey Tillotson; Engl. Studies, 15, 1933, pp. 99–105, B. A. P. van Dam; Arch. 163, 1933, S. 269–70, Werner Wokatsch; RESt. 10, 1934, pp. 353–6, Peter Alexander.
Tries to prove that Q 1 was set up from the first draft of the play much revised and F 1 from a shortened transcript of this MS.

W. W. GREG: The function of bibliography in literary criticism illustrated in a study of the text of 'King Lear'. In: Neophilologus, Jg. 18, 1933, S. 241–62.

B. A. P. VAN DAM: The text of Shakespeare's Lear. Louvain, 1935. 110 pp.= Materials for the study of the Old English drama, ed. by HENRY DE VOCHT. New Ser., vol. 10.

JOSEPH QUINCY ADAMS: The quarto of King Lear and shorthand. In: Mod. Phil., vol. 31, 1933, pp. 135–63.
Maintains that the copy used for the quarto was secured by means of shorthand.

MADELEINE DORAN: The quarto of King Lear and Bright's shorthand. In: Mod. Phil., vol. 33, 1935, pp. 139–57.

EDWARD HUBLER: The verse lining of the first quarto of King Lear. In: Parrott Presentation Volume, 1935, pp. 421–41.
Refutes the opinion that Q 1 is based on a shorthand report.

(2) LITERARY GENESIS

GIUSEPPE COCCHIARA: La leggenda di Re Lear. Torino, 1932. (161 pp.)

MADELEINE DORAN: Elements in the composition of King Lear. In: Stud. in Phil., vol. 30, 1933, pp. 34–58.

HOPE TRAVER: 'King Lear' and 'Isaiah'. In: The Sh. Assoc. Bull., vol. 9, 1934, pp. 181–5.

(3) DRAMATIC ART

CARLO PIGNONE: Il Re Lear. Discorso. Caserta, 1886. (150 pp.)

LORENZ MORSBACH: Die Eingangsszene von Shakespeares König Lear. Das Fragemotiv und seine Bedeutung. In: Nachr. Ges. Wiss. Göttingen, 1930, H. 3/4, S. 294–310.

J. S. H. BRANSOM: The tragedy of King Lear. Oxford, 1934. (227 pp.) Rev.: TLS. April 19, 1934, p. 278.

ELMER EDGAR STOLL: Kent and Gloster. In: Life and Letters, vol. 9, 1933, pp. 431–45.

(4*) Explanatory Literature

F. E. BUDD: Shakespeare, Chaucer, and Harsnett. In: RESt., vol. 11, 1935, pp. 421–9.
Concerning III. vi. 6–7.

G. B. HARRISON: The background to 'King Lear'. A time of troubles and portents. In: TLS. Dec. 28, 1935, p. 896.

(5) SUBSEQUENT HISTORY OF THE PLAY

(b) Stage-Productions

WOLFGANG DREWS: König Lear auf der deutschen Bühne im 17. und 18. Jahrhundert. Diss. Greifswald, 1931. (123 S.) Enlarged under the title: König Lear auf der deutschen Bühne bis zur Gegenwart. Berlin, 1932. (288 S.)=German. Studien, H. 114. Rev.: Zs. f. dt. Altertum u. dt. Lit. 69, 1932, S. 127–9, Winfried Klara; Bbl. 44, 1933, S. 112–13, Karl Brunner.

HELENE RICHTER: Albert Bassermanns Lear. In: Sh. Jb., Bd. 68, 1932, S. 147–50.

OTHELLO

(page 246)

(1) THE TEXT

The Bankside Shakespeare. Vol. 9: Othello [parallel impression of Q 1622 and F]. Ed. by THOMAS R. PRICE. New York, 1890. (263 pp.)

KENNETH WALTER CAMERON: Othello, quarto 1, reconsidered. In: PMLA., vol. 47, 1932, pp. 671–83.

KENNETH WALTER CAMERON: The text of Othello. An analysis. In: PMLA., vol. 49, 1934, pp. 762–96.
A complete classification of the variants between Q 1 and F 1.

(2) LITERARY GENESIS

WERNER WOKATSCH: Zur Quelle des Othello und zu Shakespeares Kenntnis des Italienischen. In: Arch., Jg. 87, Bd. 162, 1932, S. 118–19.

ANDREA DA MOSTO: Il Moro di Venezia. In: Bullettino degli studi inglesi in Italia. 1933.

J. MILTON FRENCH: Othello among the Anthropophagi. In: PMLA., vol. 49, 1934, pp. 807–9.

ALFRED HART: The date of Othello. In: TLS. Oct. 10, 1935, p. 631.

(3) SHAKESPEARE'S ART IN OTHELLO

C. HEBLER: Über die Charaktere in Shakespeares Othello. In: Neues Schweizerisches Museum, 3, 1863, S. 78–95.

FERDINAND KÖLVER: Die Beziehungen zwischen Charakter und Stil in Shakespeares Othello. Diss. Marburg, 1930. (71 S.) Rev.: JEGPh. 31, 1932, p. 433, John W. Draper.

JOHN W. DRAPER: Captain General Othello. In: Anglia, Bd. 55, 1931, S. 296–310.

JOHN W. DRAPER: 'Honest Iago'. In: PMLA., vol. 46, 1931, pp. 724–37.

JOHN W. DRAPER: Desdemona, a compound of two cultures. In: Rev. de litt. comp. 13, 1933, pp. 337–51.

JUTTA HOLTZ: Abnorme Charaktere bei Shakespeare: Othello, Richard III., Macbeth. Diss. Tübingen, 1933. (47 S.)

ELMER EDGAR STOLL: Othello the man. In: The Sh. Assoc. Bull., vol. 9, 1934, pp. 111–24.

(5) MISCELLANEOUS LITERATURE

JOHN W. DRAPER: Some details of Italian local colour in 'Othello'. In: Sh. Jb., Bd. 68, 1932, S. 125–7.

(6) SUBSEQUENT HISTORY OF THE PLAY

E. J. DUBEDOUT: Shakespeare et Voltaire. 'Othello' et 'Zaïre'. In: Mod. Phil., vol. 3, 1905/6, pp. 305–16.

GEOFFREY TILLOTSON: Othello and the Alchemist at Oxford in 1610. In: TLS. July 20, 1933, p. 494.

MACBETH
(page 247)
(2) LITERARY GENESIS

J. W. HALES: On the porter in Macbeth. In: New Sh. Soc. Trans., ser. 1, no. 2, 1874, pp. 255–84.

F. G. FLEAY: On two plays of Shakespeare's, the versions of which as we have them are the results of alterations by other hands. I. Macbeth. In: New Sh. Soc. Trans., ser. 1, no. 2, 1874, pp. 339–57.

S. R. J. ERSKINE: Mac Beth, being a sketch of the historical figure as opposed to that of some tradition and the drama. Inverness, 1930. (90 pp.)

JOHN M. ROBERTSON: Literary detection. A symposium on Macbeth. London, 1931. (173 pp.) Rev.: TLS. Nov. 5, 1931, p. 860.

ALOIS BRANDL: Zur Quelle des 'Macbeth'. In: E. St., Bd. 70, 1935, S. 169–80.

BEATRICE DAW BROWN: Exemplum materials underlying Macbeth. In: PMLA., vol. 50, 1935, pp. 700–14.

(3) DRAMATIC ART

L. PÖRSCHKE: Über Shakespeares Macbeth. Königsberg, 1801. (200 S.)

L. SCHMIDT: Macbeth, eine poetische Shakespearestudie. Oschatz, 1873. (115 S.)

ARTHUR H. GILKES: Lectures on the 'Electra' of Sophocles and 'Macbeth'. London, 1880. (xii, 148 pp.)

A. W. CRAWFORD: The apparitions in Macbeth. In: MLN., vol. 39, 1924, pp. 345–50 and 383–8.

G. WILSON KNIGHT: Macbeth and the nature of evil. In: Hibbert Journal, vol. 28, 1930, pp. 328–42.

WALTER C. CURRY: The demonic metaphysics of Macbeth. In: Stud. in Phil., vol. 30, 1933, pp. 395–426.

GREGOR VON GLASENAPP: Spuk und Prophezeihungen in Shakespeare's Macbeth. Banquo's Geist, die Hexen. In: Abhandlungen über aktuelle Fragen aus der Psychologie, Mathematik und Religion. 3. Folge. Leipzig, 1935, S. 233–74.

(3*) Art of Characterization

OTTO GILDEMEISTER: Lady Macbeth. In: Bremer Sonntagsblatt, 1863, no. 11, S. 79–88.

ALGERNON FOGGO: On the character of Banquo. In: New Sh. Soc. Trans., 1875–6, pp. 200–6.

ISIDOR HENRY CORIAT: The hysteria of Lady Macbeth. New York, 1912. (94 pp.)

R. G. MOULTON: On character development in Shakespeare as illustrated by 'Macbeth' and 'King Henry V'. In: New Sh. Soc. Trans., 1880–6, no. xxv.

JUTTA HOLTZ: Abnorme Charaktere bei Shakespeare: Othello, Richard III., Macbeth. Diss. Tübingen, 1933. (47 S.)

WALTER CLYDE CURRY: Macbeth's changing character. In: JEGPh., vol. 34, 1935, pp. 311–38.

(4) EXPLANATORY LITERATURE

H. GAUDIG: Macbeth. In his Wegweiser durch die klassischen Schuldramen. 4. Abt., Leipzig, 1899, ²1905, S. 410–66.

FRIEDRICH GUNDOLF: Shakespeares Macbeth. In: Die Horen, Jg. 5, 1928/9, S. 31–52.

ALWIN THALER: The 'lost scenes' of Macbeth. In: PMLA., vol. 49, 1934, pp. 835–47.

(6) SUBSEQUENT HISTORY OF THE DRAMA

F. G. FLEAY: Davenant's Macbeth and Shakespeare's witches. In: Anglia, Bd. 7, 1884, S. 128–44.

HEINRICH EGBRING: Johann Heinrich Voss der Jüngere als Übersetzer des 'Macbeth' von W. Shakespeare. Diss. Münster, 1911. (77 S.)

MICHAEL HOCHGESANG: Wandlungen des Dichtstils, dargestellt unter Zugrundelegung deutscher Macbeth-Übertragungen. München, 1926. (viii, 183 S.)

ANTONY AND CLEOPATRA
(page 250)
(2) LITERARY GENESIS

MARTIN ELLEHAUGE: The use of his sources made by Shakespeare in Julius Caesar and Antony and Cleopatra. In: E. St., Bd. 65, 1930/1, S. 197–210.

CORIOLANUS
(page 251)
(3) DRAMATIC ART

WALTHER SCHULZ: Shakespeares 'Coriolan' in der deutschen Shakespeare-Literatur des 19. und 20. Jahrhunderts. In: Zs. f. Deutschkunde, 1931, S. 120–7.

(4) SUBSEQUENT HISTORY OF THE PLAY

JOHANNES H. MÜLLER: J. M. R. Lenz' Coriolan. Jena, 1930. (78 S.)
Introduction and text.

TIMON OF ATHENS
(page 252)
(2) LITERARY GENESIS

WILLIAM WELLS: 'Timon of Athens'. In: N. & Q., 12th ser., vol. 6, 1920, pp. 266–9.
Asserts that the play was written by Middleton and revised by Shakespeare.

S. R. GOLDING: Timon of Athens. In: N. & Q., vol. 150, 1926, pp. 273–5; vol. 151, 1926, pp. 167–70 and 185–8.

H. DUGDALE SYKES: Timon of Athens. In: N. & Q., vol. 151, 1926, pp. 21–3.
A reply to S. R. Golding.

R. WARWICK BOND: Lucian and Boiardo in Timon of Athens. In: MLR., vol. 26, 1931, pp. 52–68.

JOHN W. DRAPER: The theme of 'Timon of Athens'. In: MLR., vol. 29, 1934, pp. 20–31.

(2*) *Miscellaneous Treatises*

SAMUEL A. TANNENBAUM: Farewell to 'Ullorxa'. In: The Sh. Assoc. Bull., vol. 11, 1936, pp. 41–5.
T. reads: 'all or ha'.

CYMBELINE

(*page 254*)

(2) LITERARY GENESIS

FRIEDRICH BRIE: Eine neue Quelle zu 'Cymbeline'? In: Sh. Jb., Jg. 44, 1908, S. 167–70.

WILLIAM FLINT THRALL: Cymbeline, Boccaccio, and the wager story in England. In: Stud. in Phil., vol. 28, 1931, pp. 639–51.

(3) DRAMATIC ART

J. W. MACKAIL: Mother and son in 'Cymbeline'. In: A book of homage to Shakespeare, ed. by ISRAEL GOLLANCZ. London, 1916, pp. 193–6.

WENDELL MAGEE KECK: Accounting for irregularities in Cloten. In: The Sh. Assoc. Bull., vol. 10, 1935, pp. 67–72.

(3*) *Miscellaneous Treatises*

SAMUEL A. TANNENBAUM: Shakspere's caste prejudices. A reply to Ernest Crosby. In his Shaksperian scraps and other Elizabethan fragments. New York, 1933, pp. 153–76.

(4) SUBSEQUENT HISTORY OF THE PLAY

Imogen. Märchendrama von Shakespeare. Für die deutsche Bühne übertragen von HANS OLDEN. Berlin, 1931. (187 S.)

GERHART GÖHLER: Grundzüge der Regie und Dramaturgie einer neuen Bühnenbearbeitung von Shakespeares Cymbelin. Dresden, 1932. (32 S.)

GERHART GÖHLER: Zum Bühnenproblem des 'Cymbelin'. In: Sh. Jb., Bd. 69, 1933, S. 131–65.

THE WINTER'S TALE

(*page 255*)

(1) THE TEXT

SAMUEL A. TANNENBAUM: Ralph Crane and The Winter's Tale. In his Shaksperian scraps and other Elizabethan fragments. New York, 1933, pp. 75–86.

(2) LITERARY GENESIS

KARL FRIES: Quellenstudien zu Shakespeares Wintermärchen. In: Neue Jbb. f. d. klass. Altertum. Jg. 3, 1900, S. 557–65.

THE TEMPEST
(*page 256*)
(2) LITERARY GENESIS

JOHANNES MEISSNER: Untersuchungen über Shakespeares 'Sturm'. Dessau, 1872. (vii, 151 S.)

(2*) *Art of Characterization*

MARIE H. STURGISS: Shakspere's Miranda. In: The Sh. Assoc. Bull., vol. 10, 1935, pp. 36–44.

HANS NEUHOF: Die Calibangestalt in Shakespeares Sturm. In: GRM., Jg. 23, 1935, S. 116–28.

(3) EXPLANATORY LITERATURE

R. G. MOULTON: Shakespeare's 'Tempest' as an illustration of the theory of central ideas. In: Trans. New Sh. Soc., 1887–92, no. II.

SAMUEL A. TANNENBAUM: Textual difficulties in The Tempest, old and new. In: The Sh. Assoc. Bull., vol. 6, 1931, pp. 148–60. Rev.: ibid., pp. 186–91, Hoxie Neale Fairchild.

NELSON SHERWIN BUSHNELL: Natural supernaturalism in The Tempest. In: PMLA., vol. 47, 1932, pp. 684–98.

WALTER CLYDE CURRY: Sacerdotal science in Shakespeare's 'The Tempest'. In: Arch., Jg. 90, Bd. 168, 1935, S. 25–36 and S. 185–96.

(4) SYMBOLISM

ELMER EDGAR STOLL: The Tempest. In: PMLA., vol. 47, 1932, pp. 699–726. S. 'cannot believe that there is any allegory, or symbolism, or even veiled biography in the play'.

KING HENRY VIII
(*page 259*)
(I) LITERARY GENESIS

W. J. LAWRENCE: The stage directions in 'King Henry VIII'. In: TLS. Dec. 18, 1930, p. 1085. Cf. also: TLS. Jan. 1, 1931, p. 12.

PETER ALEXANDER: Conjectural history, or, Shakespeare's Henry VIII. In: Essays and Studies, vol. 16, 1931, pp. 85–120.

CUMBERLAND CLARK: A study of Shakespeare's Henry VIII. London, 1931. (218 pp.)

PERICLES
(*page 260*)
(I) THE TEXT

The Bankside Shakespeare. Vol. 14: Pericles [parallel impression of Q 1609 and F 3]. Ed. by APPLETON MORGAN. New York, 1891. (li, 249 pp.)

Marina. A dramatic romance by Shakespeare, being the Shakespearian portion of the tragedy of 'Pericles', ed. by S. WELLWOOD. London, 1902. (48 pp.)

WILLIAM PETERFIELD TRENT: Some textual notes on 'Pericles'. In: Shakespearian Studies, ed. by B. MATTHEWS and A. H. THORNDIKE. New York, 1916, pp. 45-57.

(2) LITERARY GENESIS

SINA SPIKER: George Wilkins and the authorship of Pericles. In: Stud. in Phil., vol. 30, 1933, pp. 551-70.
Evidence against Wilkins being one of the collaborators in Pericles.

III. SHAKESPEARE'S POEMS

(1) SHAKESPEARE'S POEMS IN GENERAL

(b) GERMAN TRANSLATIONS

(page 262)

William Shakespeares sämtliche lyrische Gedichte, übersetzt von GOTTLIEB REGIS. In: Shakespeare-Almanach, hrsg. v. GOTTLIEB REGIS. Berlin, 1836. (358 S.)

ALBERT RITTER: Der unbekannte Shakespeare. Eine Auswahl aus Shakespeares Werken. Berlin, 1923. (302 S.)

(c) TREATISES

(page 263)

FRIEDRICH KREYSSIG: Shakespeares lyrische Gedichte und ihre neuesten deutschen Bearbeiter. I, II. In: Preuss. Jbb., Jg. 13, 1864, S. 484-504 u. Jg. 14, 1864, S. 91-114.

W. STEUERWALD: Lyrisches im Shakspere. München, 1881. (161 S.)

LORENZ MORSBACH: Shakespeares Epen und Sonette. In: Shakespeares Werke. Übertr. nach Schlegel-Tieck von MAX J. WOLFF. Berlin, 1926, Bd. 22, S. 203-40.

GEORGE RYLANDS: Shakespeare the poet. In: A companion to Shakespeare studies. C.U.P., 1934, pp. 89-115.

(2) THE SONNETS

(a) ENGLISH EDITIONS

(page 263)

The sonnets of William Shakespeare, re-arranged and divided into four parts, with an introduction and explanatory notes (by Dr. R. CARTWRIGHT). London, 1859. (120 pp.)

J. A. FORT: A time scheme for Shakespeare's sonnets, with a text and short notes. London, 1929. (150 pp.) Rev.: RESt. 6, 1930, pp. 467-9, P. Alexander.
Considers the arrangement in Q 1609 to be chronologically correct. Fr.=Southampton. R.P.=Chapman.

ALFRED DOUGLAS: The true history of Shakespeare's sonnets. London, 1933. (216 pp.)

(b) GERMAN TRANSLATIONS

(page 264)

LUDWIG W. KAHN: Shakespeares Sonette in Deutschland. Versuch einer literarischen Typologie. Bern, 1935. (122 S.) Rev.: MLR. 31, 1936, pp. 253–4, J. Shawcross.

Shakespeares Southampton-Sonette. Deutsch von FRITZ KRAUSS. Leipzig, 1872.

William Shakespeares Lied an die Schönheit. Eine Übertragung der Sonette von BEATRICE BARNSTORFF-FRAME. Paderborn, 1931. (183 S.)

Shakespeares Sonette. Nachdichtung von KARL KRAUS. Wien, 1933. (81 Bl.)

RICHARD FLATTER: Karl Kraus als Nachdichter Shakespeares. Eine sprach-kritische Untersuchung. Wien, 1933. (87 S.)

Shakespeares Sonette. Englisch und Deutsch. Übertr. von RICHARD FLATTER. Wien, 1934. (167 S.) Rev.: Bbl. 46, 1935, S. 117–18, W. Fischer.

(b*) TRANSLATIONS INTO OTHER GERMANIC LANGUAGES

Shakespeares sonnetten, met inleiding en aanteekeningen door J. DECROOS. Kortrijk, 1933. (113 pp.)

Shakespeares sonnetten, nagedicht door ALBERT VERWEY. Santpoort, 1933. (176 pp.)

(c) TREATISES

(page 265)

B. R. WARD: The mystery of 'Mr. W. H.' London, 1923. (viii, 133 pp.)

SIDNEY LEE: Ovid and Shakespeare's sonnets. In his Elizabethan and other essays. O.U.P., 1929, pp. 116–39.

H. HARVEY WOOD: A 17th century MS. of poems by Donne and others. In: Essays and Studies by members of the Engl. Assoc., vol. 16, 1931, pp. 179–90. Contains a version of Shakespeare's 2nd sonnet, which differs considerably from the 1609 print.

LEON KELLNER: Shakespeares Sonette. In: E. St., Bd. 68, 1933, S. 57–80.

GARRETT MATTINGLY: The date of Shakespeare's sonnet CVII. In: PMLA., vol. 48, 1933, pp. 705–21.

FRIEDRICH DANNENBERG: Shakespeares Sonette: Herkunft, Wesen, Deutung. In: Sh. Jb., Bd. 70, 1934, S. 37–64.

L. E. PEARSON: Elizabethan love conventions. Berkeley, Univ. of Calif. Pr., 1933. (xi, 365 pp.) Deals with the sonnet cycles of the last two decades of the sixteenth century and with the reaction against Petrarchism.

(3) SHAKESPEARE'S EPIC POEMS

(b) VENUS AND ADONIS

(page 269)

HAZELTON SPENCER: Shakespeare's use of Golding in 'Venus and Adonis'. In: MLN., vol. 44, 1929, pp. 435–7.

H. T. S. FORREST: The original Venus and Adonis. London, 1930. (132 pp.)
Rev.: Rev. anglo-amér. 8, 1931, p. 438, A. Koszul.

(c) THE RAPE OF LUCRECE

(page 270)

Shakespeare's *Lukretia*. Übertr. von FRIEDRICH BODENSTEDT. In: ALBERT
RITTER: Der unbekannte Shakespeare. Berlin, 1923, S. 53–114.

SIDNEY COLVIN: The sack of Troy in Shakespeare's Lucrece and in some 15th
century drawings and tapestries. In: A book of homage to Shakespeare, ed.
by ISRAEL GOLLANCZ. London, 1916, pp. 88–99.

WILHELM MARSCHALL: Das Troja-Gemälde in Shakespeares 'Lucrece'. In:
Anglia, Bd. 54, N.F., Bd. 42, 1930, S. 83–96.

HANS GALINSKY: Der Lucretia-Stoff in der Weltliteratur. Diss. Breslau,
1932. (234 S.)

(4) SHAKESPEARE'S LYRIC POEMS

(a) A LOVER'S COMPLAINT

(page 270)

GREGOR SARRAZIN: Über Shakespeares Klage der Liebenden = Kleine Shakespeare-Studien II. In: Beitr. z. roman. u. engl. Philologie. Dem 10. Dt.
Neuphilologentage überreicht. Breslau, 1902, S. 197–211.

(c) THE PHOENIX AND THE TURTLE

(page 271)

Ranjee: Towards the stars. With an introd. by EDWARD GARNETT and an
appreciation by ANDRÉ MAUROIS. No place [1931]. 64 pp.

Deals with the Phoenix and the Turtle, and suggests Fletcher as the probable author
of the poem.

MAX J. WOLFF: Zum 'Phoenix and Turtle'. In: E. St., Bd. 67, 1932, S. 159.

IV. THE SHAKESPEARE APOCRYPHA

(1) THE SHAKESPEARE APOCRYPHA IN GENERAL

(b) GERMAN TRANSLATIONS

(page 271)

Altenglisches Theater, oder Supplemente zum Shakspear. Übers. und hrsg.
von LUDWIG TIECK. 2 Bde. Berlin, 1811. (xxiii, 371 u. xiv, 348 S.)
Containing: King John (old play), George-a-Green, Per., Locr., Merry D., Leir (old
play).

(b*) TRANSLATIONS INTO OTHER LANGUAGES

Opere attribuite a Shakespeare, a cura di DIEGO ANGELI. 2 vol. Milano, 1934 =
Shakespeare, Teatro completo. Vol. 39/40.
Containing: I. Yorksh., Arden, Kins. II. Locr., Prod. S., Edw. III.

(c) TREATISES

(page 272)

RICHARD SIMPSON: On some plays attributed to Shakspere. In: New Sh. Soc. Trans., 1875-6, pp. 155-80.

(2) THE INDIVIDUAL PLAYS

ARDEN OF FEVERSHAM

(page 272)

W. J. LAWRENCE: The authorship of Arden. In: TLS. June 28, 1934, p. 460.

LOCRINE

(page 273)

SAMUEL A. TANNENBAUM: A Locrine forgery. In his Shaksperian scraps and other Elizabethan fragments. New York, 1933, pp. 36-41.

KING EDWARD III

(page 273)

William Shakespeare: Grevinden af Salisbury og Marina. Oversatte og kommenterede af V. ØSTERBERG. Kopenhagen, 1926. (94 pp.)

ALFRED HART: The vocabulary of Edward III. In his Shakespeare and the homilies. O.U.P., 1934, pp. 219-41.

THE LONDON PRODIGAL SON

(page 275)

Der Taugenichts (The London Prodigall). Übertr. von ERNST ORTLEPP und ALBERT RITTER. In: Albert Ritter's Der unbekannte Shakespeare. Berlin, 1923, S. 115-209.

William Shakespeare: Der Londoner verlorene Sohn. Dt. Bearb. von ERNST KAMNITZER. Hellerau, 1930. (224 S.)

ADOLF SCHWECKENDIEK: Bühnengeschichte des Verlorenen Sohnes in Deutschland. T. 1: 1527-1627. Leipzig, 1930. (xv, 163 S.)

A YORKSHIRE TRAGEDY

(page 275)

Ein Trauerspiel in Yorkshire. Übertr. v. ALBERT RITTER. In his Der unbekannte Shakespeare. Berlin, 1923, S. 211-45.

FAIR EM

(page 275)

ALWIN THALER: Faire Em (and Shakspere's Company?) in Lancashire. In: PMLA., vol. 46, 1931, pp. 647-58.

THE TWO NOBLE KINSMEN

(*page 275*)

HENRY DAVID GRAY: Beaumont and 'The Two Noble Kinsmen'. In: Phil. Quart., vol. 2, 1923, pp. 112-31.

A. C. BRADLEY: Scene-endings in Shakespeare and in 'The Two Noble Kinsmen'. In his A miscellany. London, 1929, pp. 218-24.

ALFRED HART: Shakespeare and the vocabulary of 'The Two Noble Kinsmen'. In: RESt., vol. 10, 1934, pp. 274-87. Also in his Shakespeare and the homilies. O.U.P., 1934, pp. 242-56.
Holds that the play should be included in the Shakespeare canon.

THE BOOK OF SIR THOMAS MORE

(*page 277*)

Sir Thomas More. German translation by MAX J. WOLFF. In: Shakespeares Werke. Übertr. nach Schlegel-Tieck von MAX J. WOLFF. Bd. 21. Berlin, 1926. (153 S.)

SAMUEL A. TANNENBAUM: Shakespeare and 'Sir Thomas Moore'. New York and London, 1929. (64 pp.) Rev.: Rev. anglo-amér. 8, 1930, pp. 228-31, M. Praz; MLN. 46, 1931, pp. 192-4, R. S. Forsythe; E. St. 66, 1931, S. 121-2, Ed. Eckhardt.

CAROLINE F. E. SPURGEON: Imagery in the Sir Thomas More fragment. In: RESt., vol. 6, 1930, pp. 257-70.

R. W. CHAMBERS: Some sequences of thought in Shakespeare and in the 147 lines of 'Sir Thomas More'. In: MLR., vol. 26, 1931, pp. 251-80. Rev.: Bbl. 44, 1933, S. 114-16, A. Eichler.

MARIE SCHÜTT: Die Quellen des 'Book of Sir Thomas More'. In: E. St., Bd. 68, 1933, S. 209-26.

D. C. COLLINS: On the date of Sir Thomas More. In: RESt., vol. 10, 1934, pp. 401-11.
Assumes a date about 1601.

INDEX